THE FINAL FRONTIER

Leadership actions for young
and aspiring leaders

Ronnie Francis

ISBN: 978-967-14746-0-0 First pubished in print in Malaysia 2017
Publlished as a digital edition on Amazon Kindle in 2021
ISBN: 9798755417280 Paperback edition published 2021
email: dicomronnie@gmail.com

To Almighty God, my heavenly Father

To my beloved wife Kiran, my best friend in life

*To my son Andrew & my daughter Angela, my
greatest achievement in this life*

CONTENTS

FOREWORD

The idea for this book began three years ago when I was asked to co-write a project management manual for young project managers. The seed of which was sown in the idiom that I coined for performing right actions for successful project management. The idiom leaderactions has grown into this book comprising leadershipactions. Each chapter is made up of actions from this idiom making it catchy enough for the reader to remember and contains the right actions required for the every day leader which is in you and me. It is hoped that as the reader reads each chapter, it will lead to a better understanding of oneself and appreciate the nature of each and every one of us. To come to the realization that though we may look very different from the outside we are all not that very different at all on the inside. Hence let us start by learning to accept and understand ourselves first, so that we can better understand those around us.

This book was written with this in mind and it is the hope of the writer that it will help all who read it, create a new and exciting world of the future. A world where the good and noble will prevail.

The writer believes that the key to success and happiness lies within each and every one of us. It is left to us to find with humility the right recipe for our own success and happiness.

So go ahead and start by turning to the next page and start your journey to the final frontier...yourself!

VIII

INTRODUCTION

Man is ever looking outwards to discover new worlds, new life forms and new inventions. The universe is so vast and unending. Mankind has only just begun to scrape the outer reaches of our solar system. Even the oceans remain a mystery with its vast and hidden mountains and canyons. This makes us wonder how little we know of the world around us, how little we know of our own selves especially our human mind. The human mind is in itself a wonder of creation and still remains a great mystery. It is akin to the depths of the oceans and the vastness of the universe. Each of us is, not unlike, a solar system by itself. Should we not be looking within ourselves to unlock the mysteries and still untapped potentials that we as yet do not know? We know for a fact that we utilize only a small fraction of our minds potential. The rest is still untapped and remains a mystery.

We hear of individuals who claim they have powers which allow them to do mind boggling stuff which can leave you in disbelief. Have they somehow developed their minds to achieve this ability or are they just cleverly orchestrated tricks to deceive us. What we don't understand we call magic. There are mystics, sages, conjurists or magicians who can walk on hot coals, levitate in the air and even sleep on sharp nails. Have they developed their minds to overcome the physical self? Hence isn't it apt to say that the human mind is in fact the final frontier, since if we can unlock the powers within our minds, can we then not be able to transcend the depths of the oceans or the vastness of the universe itself?

But for now let's get back to reality and look at the world today. We are now living in a world which is undergoing great changes. The twentieth century dawned with the industrial revolution and saw the advent of the information age and rush to computerization. Towards the last quarter of that century dawned the birth of biotechnology and miniaturization with microchips. Now in the twenty-first century and in just a few short years, we have witnessed the dawn of the new technological revolution. Bulky desktop computers have evolved to laptops and now into hand-held light weight smartphones and even Dick Tracy like smart phone watches. This new age mini wonder has been embraced by both the young and the old alike.

Today you can see almost everyone holding a smartphone to communicate, carry out banking activities, take photographs, book airline tickets, make hotel reservations, advertise products, watch movies, study online, play games or listen to their favourite music, among others, with the tap of a finger whilst sitting in the comfort of the home over a cup of coffee. In the world of business environment, businesses can carry out most business activities with the use of such devices to the extent that issuing employees with such devices is no longer the preview of top management but is now a norm and a necessity for all levels of executives and even non-executives and is integral for the success of today's businesses. Being hardwired has become the trend. People everywhere in the world today are connected together in a communications network that is beyond the control of any government. You don't need anyone to tell you anything about anything anymore, since everyone is empowered through this sophisticated communication network. People can see or read about what's happening in the rest of the world at anytime as the news unravels.

The business environment today has grown dramatically more intense, with globalized competition and technology speeding on with great innovation. The following are some articles which have been quoted to show the speed with which technology is indeed travelling:

> There are reports that Google, with the help of NASA, have developed a quantum computer. This would be the first giant leap to creating Artificial Intelligence or A.I. for short. Could we be on the threshold of seeing a Jarvis, Tony Stark's A.I. digital assistant in the movie Iron Man. The D-Wave 2x, Google's quantum computer, is 100 times faster that the fastest computer today. The D-Wave will the have the power to store, catalogue, and analyse vast amounts of data and provide solutions. -Jason Godfrey

> In the Medical field, urologists and neurosurgeons are increasingly performing robot-assisted operations. Gradually, operations in body cavities-in the abdomen or chest-won't require you to be opened up anymore, but will become minimally invasive using robot-controlled systems. In these operations, the surgeon sits at a console several meters away from the operating table and controls-via a robotic arm-miniature instruments such as scissors and needle inside the patient's body. The surgeon can operate with extremely high maneuverability and is aided by 3D images- magnified up to 10 times-provided by a special camera to monitor. The future would be "augmented reality", in which a diagnostic image-for example a marked tumour-would be projected into the operation image. The operating surgeon will then know exactly where the tumour is hidden and remove it without destroying healthy brain tissue. In a world first, robot-assisted casualty surgery is being performed at Kiel University hospital.

> Specialized robotic devices that assume service tasks such as sterilizing surgical instruments are also conceivable. Already in use at hospital wards, are robotic transport systems that distribute food to beds, clear away trays and drive themselves into the robotic kitchen. -Yuriko Wahl-Immel

Leaders today can no longer just issue orders and expect employees to mindlessly obey. Personal relationships can no longer be just taken for granted. The great new age failure is that though people have the empowerment today to communicate, they fail to do so and they are failing to do so in every area whether at home or at the workplace. In Japan, this failure has given birth to a new industry. Robotic pets and humanoids have started taking the place of human relationship in many homes of elderly people who have to cope with this new age disease called loneliness.

The Mind of man has created all these technological wonders. Human beings are heralding a new digital age. However with all these inventions and marvels, mankind is still embroiled in destructive behaviour. Escalation in brutal violence and conflict especially in terrorist acts has seen the deaths of hundreds of thousands of innocent people in recent times. If the mind is where the seed is formed, then the field where that seed is sown is our hearts and it is in our hearts that the wheat and the weeds are found. So, how do we deal with them?

Recalling a popular Native American tale can help: An elderly Native American was teaching his grandchildren about life, saying, "There is a fight going on inside me. It is a terrible fight and it is between two wolves. One wolf is bad and evil-he creates anger, fear, envy, despair, greed, arrogance, guilt, lies, false pride, resentment, and competition in me. The other is good and noble-he generates love, faith, peace, joy, hope, humility, kindness, friendship, generosity, truthfulness, and compassion in me. You too have this same fight going on inside you. In fact, this fight goes on inside every person on earth." The children thought about it for a moment and then one of them asked, "Which wolf will win in the end, grandpa?" The grandfather replied, "The one you feed."

The leaders of this new cultural or digital revolution or whatever you may wish to call it, will have to establish a real vision and a sense of values within organizations they wish to lead and manage conditions of almost constant change. Technology alone is never enough, however. Hence those businesses which understand the importance of human relationships and the need to hone their employees' skills to become better will make a big difference in the success or failure of their businesses. Good human relationship skills have the ability to change managers into leaders. We need to create and nurture good values within ourselves to become better leaders within our organizations, in our family life and with society as a whole for building a better world. A world built on a more caring and sustainable economic system with citizens, business leaders and politicians working together. Only then can we overcome the challenges that this world faces today on so many fronts.

JUST WHAT I NEED......
I'LL TAKE TWO
THIS MACHINE WILL DO HALF THE WORK FOR YOU....
SALE
RONNIE

CHAPTER 1-
LEAD BY EXAMPLE

"Walk the talk"

In 1990, I joined a newly established oil company which had just been set up in Pasir Gudang, in the state of Johor in Malaysia. The company was led by a very dynamic General Manager (GM) with very unstinting principles. The examples set by him were a great source of inspiration to employees even till today.

A good leader sets good examples. Such leaders do so not because of the title they hold or the salary they earn. What made this particular GM a leader of men and women was how he interacted with all levels of personnel. He recognized the need to help people achieve what they were capable of and to establish a vision for the future of the business. He encouraged and mentored by the examples that he set and established and maintained a very successful relationship with his staff.

A leader does not need to do great things, he leads by doing little things in a great way. He would arrive at work very early. He would then start his daily regimen by starting his daily walk around the work sites, at 7.30 in the morning, when many employees would still be walking in or driving into the work site. He would do the same right after lunch break and prior to the end of each working day. Due to his good example of showing staff the importance of timeliness in work, timeliness and productivity improved. He walked the talk.

On another occasion, while at the top of a structure under construction, supervising the installation of a vital component, I felt a light tap on my shoulder. Being so high up and surrounded by the noise, dirt, heat and also a little bit tired, I turned around and was pleasantly surprised to see the GM in person. He pulled me aside and asked about the progress. After a light chat he then continued with his normal rounds. This impression set on a young engineers' mind remains with me to this day. When I became part of senior management I too would do my daily rounds to meet and greet personnel under me. Managers under him would need to give him accurate progress reports since he also had first-hand information. He knew the importance of good interpersonal skills, good communication and building strong teams for the success of the business he was leading. He walked the talk and set good examples for his future leaders to follow.

Securing more contracts from satisfied customers became a norm, even though there were other competitors who could offer the same or more services. What separated us from the rest was the culture of our employees. Customers felt comfortable dealing with our employees. They knew that we understood what they really cared about, what they wanted and showed them how easily they could have their requirements satisfied.

The leader had nurtured the employees to exceed customer expectations. By doing this he knew that customers would come back again and again… and they did over and over again and the company order book grew. By always seeing things from the customers' perspective, we will discover what is most important in their eyes and help to continuously grow our business whether large or small. Such leaders existed even during those times when businesses operated in a stable environment.

During the 80's and 90's, oil prices were very stable and were high enough for oil companies to easily rake in 20 percent profit margins. USD 100 - 120 per barrel of oil was not uncommon. There was optimism within the oil industry, and great concern in others, that oil prices could even hit the USD 200 per barrel mark. But today's business environments have become volatile. Businesses are now sailing in unchartered waters and require flexibility.

Great leadership skills are now required more than ever before. Taking the oil companies as an example, oil prices are now, fluctuating at around USD 80 per barrel from USD 50 per barrel where they had been languishing for so long. This is not because demands have increased but rather due to global production and supply chain disruptions. Profit margins have dropped from the highs of 20 per cent in the 90's. Achieving a profit margin of 5 per cent is considered enough to survive in the business today. The great strides taking place especially in the energy efficiency and substitutions to oil has seen the dependence and subsequent demand on oil going down. Renewable energy and other technological strides such as electric cars continue with their rapid advance. Many oil companies have started to downsize. There are reports that some of the world's largest energy companies, believe demand for oil could peak sooner than expected, a rare statement in an industry that commonly forecasts decades of growth.

Retrenchment is rife in the industry. Many companies are not ready for it. They are realizing that as they downsize operations to increase productivity, that employees with human relationship skills are what are required to survive. People having good interpersonal skills, able to communicate, able to step aside and see what's important to customers and build teams will become the leaders of today and tomorrow. Such leaders will help achieve the vision for businesses to survive and sustain their business environment.

BOSS, PEOPLE SAY YOU'RE A MANAGER WHO HASN'T MOVED WITH THE TIMES.
BAH! NONSENSE! HANG ON, I NEED TO CHECK THE FIGURES WITH MY ABACUS, FOR YOU!!
MANAGER
RONNIE

CHAPTER 2-

ENCOURAGING GOOD COMMUNICATION

"Don't let communication, or the lack of it, get you down"

One of the greatest failures of our century is the failure to communicate. Though we have invented a wide array of technological devices and communication tools together with the software to use them with, weakness in communication skills is today the single most important element which is negatively impacting our daily lives.

Communicating by directly speaking to the person rather than communicating via countless text messages via WhatsApp or through Twitter and Facebook is immensely more valuable. We have lost the human touch in communicating effectively with each other.

In business, the use of emails to send information and communicate messages is vital to keeping the whole organization hardwired and connected together. Everyone, from the CEO, top management, middle and line managers, engineers and departmental secretaries and clerks have at least a desktop computer on their tables. We are, most of our working hours, staring at the screen and analyzing the immense amounts of data and information which are coming in every minute of our working hours and even after we clock off. What this causes is the lack of direct interaction between staff in different units within the same organization and increases the level of stress within ourselves. Lack of interaction invariably leads to failure to communicate and this then creates arguments and conflicts within the organization. Many times a manager's precious time is used up with managing conflicts which could have otherwise been resolved right away if employees had only applied direct communication with each other.

Communication is not just about speaking. In fact according to psychological studies, words make up only 7 per cent of communication. The tone of our voice makes up 38 per cent of it while 55 per cent of communication is by body language. Tone and action may convey up to 93 per cent of our thoughts and feelings to the people with whom we communicate. Whether communicating at home with our children, with our spouse, with the people at our work place or at social gatherings, we must understand and be aware of ourselves. Being self aware in the manner in which we speak, by the words that we choose to use, and the tone of our voice and our body language will help to decide the outcome of whatever subject that we are discussing with anyone.

I was working as an interface manager on a project which required me to be stationed at the Design Engineering Consultant office. The employees, who were mostly highly qualified engineers, were seated within cubicles separated by half partitions. Hence everyone could see each other clearly and be able to interact better. I too was seated at a cubicle in between two other engineers. After a week on the job, I noticed that both these engineers were not interacting or even exchanging any conversation with each other, even though I was exchanging light conversation with both of them. After two weeks, their supervisor arrived at their workstations and summoned both of them to her office. Later I came to know that both these engineers had been having some misunderstanding over some issue and had started an email 'war' between one another. It was by pure chance that one of them had included the supervisor in the emails which allowed the supervisor to come down and stop and manage the conflict.

If both engineers had taken the initiative to speak directly to one another and resolve their differences, the workplace would have been a much better and productive place to be in. This is most often the case in many units and departments and organizations.

We need to put the art of good communication back into our organizations. Failure to communicate has become the greatest failure of this century. As leaders we need to listen so as to learn. Listening is also another important part of the art of good communication. No one can possibly know everything. Dale Carnegie in his book *The Leader in You* said: "Listening to others is the single best way to learn and improve your communication with your employees and between employees."
Quoting from J.Maurus in *The Joy of Being Human*:

> Silence, too, is a notable part in communication. It is important in listening as well as in any conversation. Too many listeners are quick to jump in and interrupt the flow of thought just as soon as a person stops talking. Give time to the person to talk more fully. Silence favors the thinking. It puts the talker at ease to remarshal his thoughts and pursue his subject with more clarity. Silence at the right point of time in the conversation enables both the talker and the listener to remain calm and attain more clarity of thought. It serves as a great self-discipline and gives life and order to the flow of words.

People love to be listened to, and almost always respond to others who listen to them. A good listener can become a very persuasive leader. Listening facilitates understanding and the ability to ask the right questions. Responding to questions quickly and directly and finally ensuring that your employees feel that they are being listened to actively. All these will improve the overall communication within an organization.

As a trained Accident Investigator, I often get called on to carry out accident investigation in the event of any accidents within the oil and gas fabrication yard. One very good example which showcases the impact of poor communication could be shown by the following example of how poor communication resulted in a major accident.

In the year 2005, a massive steel jacket structure was being readied for sail away operations at the jetty. Jackets are the offshore substructures of an offshore oil and gas platform and they are the foundation on which the topside superstructures are placed. This particular jacket had been loaded onto an oceangoing barge. The oceangoing tug had already been hooked up for towing the jacket barge and was secured to the portside of the barge. On the starboard side were two harbor tugs to assist till the handover point. The sail away operation was in the capable hands of a very experienced harbor pilot. All three tugboat captains and the pilot used walkie-talkie communication devices for giving and receiving instructions. All communication was conducted in the English language.

Prior to the operation, a safety briefing was held between all the four teams. The operation began with the pilot giving the command to slowly move ahead. The Jacket barge started to move ahead. Things seemed to be going according to plan. As the barge cleared the safe distance from the jetty, the pilot then gave the second command… "all ahead full". As all three tugboats revved up their throttles, the Jacket barge, however started to slow down, turn and move back towards the jetty from which it had come from. Before the pilot could react to this sudden and alarming situation, the jacket barge had picked up speed and was now heading on a direct collision course with the jetty. The pilot then gave the only command he could at that point of time and that was to stop all engines. However it was too late, since the jacket barge, moving under its own momentum, had become a juggernaut heading directly to the jetty from which it had sailed from.

Close by, on the jetty, was a topside superstructure still under construction. On the day of this sail away operation, there were many personnel including young management trainees, on top of this structure and on the ground observing the sail away operation, unaware of the drama that was unfolding. Many panicked and were shocked on seeing the behemoth approaching on a collision course with the jetty. The impact, when it happened, was great and part of the jacket structure tore into the topside causing it to heave and sway alarmingly. Many of the personnel were at that point running, helter-skelter, down the stairways to reach the ground and many were injured, but none seriously thankfully. Both the barge and the jetty together with the topside structure were also heavily damaged.

We were very lucky that no one was killed or badly injured and we got away with just shocked and lightly injured personnel, some of whom were treated for psychological trauma. The topside superstructure could very well have been toppled with serious injuries or great loss of life to the personnel on it. So what really happened and could this unfortunate incident have been avoided?

After spending two days, interviewing all the personnel involved and studying sketches of the sail away operation and the technical data of the tugs involved, three things became very clear. The first was that the captain of the oceangoing tug could not understand English and the instruction was interpreted to him by his assistant. The second, was that the oceangoing tug was more powerful than both the harbor tugs combined and the third and final factor being that the oceangoing tug was tied to the portside with its bow facing the jetty while both harbor tugs were facing the opposite direction. The pilot had given the same instruction to all three tug boat captains. The captain of the oceangoing tug and both the captains of the two harbor tugs received the instruction to move forward, which they did. The pilot should have given two sets of commands rather than one, taking into consideration that all tugs were not facing the same direction.

Hence the powerful oceangoing tug had the capacity to pull the combined weight of the barge and the other two tugs towards the opposite direction and the momentum of the barge did the rest and the accident happened. So communication failure was identified as the main root cause of the accident together with other indirect causes.

Always encourage good communication. In communication there is much more than speaking and listening. Spoken messages, for example, are accompanied by non-verbal cues, which often have more significance than what is actually said. One prerequisite of good communication is the consistent use of communication skills. Expressing our thoughts, needs and feelings clearly is a skill. To express ourselves effectively, we must learn how to put what we want to convey into a clear and understandable language.

Sincere, open and empathetic communication will convey your feelings and needs more effectively. The manner in which a person speaks will always lead to either a helpful or unhelpful dialogue with the other. A person in dialogue must be able to respond with his or her whole person, at both the physical and emotional levels. If one accuses, evaluates, moralizes or judges the other, a defensive climate is created, forcing the other to find reasons to save face thus blocking genuine communication. Each would degenerate into justifying their stand without being open to the other. Dialogue must be helpful and needs discipline against wanting to be always in the right. One must be ready to be challenged by the reality and be willing to change.

Suppose a couple is going to an important wedding function and the car cannot start. The wife gets irritated and retorts, "Why didn't you check the car before this. I told you we needed to be there on time. Now we will miss the wedding altogether. You have no consideration for me?" This sounds like the husband is being accused of being shoddy and may cause him to feel annoyed and may even spoil the enjoyment of going for the function together with his wife. If, however the wife had understood and accepted the situation and gently said, "Let's just take a cab, dear, and you can check the car tomorrow. We can still make the function on time." This would make the husband feel that his wife understood the situation and was thinking in a caring manner. They would then not only have a good evening but their relationship would grow stronger and become more closer. James Aril SJ says the following in his book *Be At Your Best*:

> Criticism always decides. Appreciation, however always unites. Nagging and negative criticism are sure ways of digging your own friendship grave. When criticism is necessary, it must be done in a constructive manner by communicating your acceptance of the other in spite of their faults. Trivialities are at the bottom of most marital unhappiness and is the main cause of many divorce cases. Trivial things like a kind word, well-timed gesture of love, or a small birthday gift are the openings of the never-ending vista of living and growing together happily.

Never underestimate the power of having good communication. Your life and the lives of others will be better for it. Your life and the lives of others may also depend on it!

HERE'S THE LATEST ICEBERG SIGHTING REPORT... SIR!
THANK YOU... BETTER LATE THAN NEVER!
WE JUST HIT AN ICEBERG... SHE WON'T SINK, WILL SHE CAPTAIN?
WHAT WAS THAT?
ICEBERG.

CHAPTER 3-
ACHIEVING BALANCE
IN LIFE

"Be the architect of yourself"

In this chapter we will learn that achieving balance in life is the single most important thing that you need to do in order to have a more happier and more satisfying personal life and also make you more energetic, more focused and more productive at work. To be a good leader, you need to have all aspects of your life and not just your work life to be healthy and in a strong state.

Many of today's modern organizations realize the importance of having well-rounded people who are able to balance not only their work but also other aspects of their personal lives. The most important being to be able to get along with their spouse, bring up their children well and also get along with the people they work with in general, without which any executive will not be able to make good decisions and be successful in succeeding in or for the organization.

Leaders who are workaholics and have only one single dimension in their lives and focus twenty-four seven on their careers, ultimately will have their mental and physical health affected and have a negative impact on the lives of those who work with them.

It is therefore vital for us to balance out our lives and make space for other things other than work.

It was always thought that hard work leads to success and success leads to happiness, right? Wrong! It is now believed that happiness leads to hard work and hard work leads to success. Happiness is a daily conscious decision which everyone needs to focus on. A leader who is able to achieve emotional stability and peace and grow spiritually will live longer, healthier and be happier.The human persona is made up of three dimensions, viz., the intelligence quotient (IQ), the emotional quotient (EQ) and the spiritual quotient (SQ). There is a wise saying, "Growing old is mandatory, growing up is optional". A mature leader will grow and becomes a more stable and balanced person as he or she grows older and be able to take better control of their lives. We not only need to accept the fact that we can't stop getting older, but know that we need to grow emotionally, spiritually and become more wiser and knowledgeable with age. The Japanese have a strict policy in which the head of a company, in addition to his experience, skills and talents, must also be of a certain age bracket, since an older leader is believed to be a more stable and balanced person to lead the organization and make the right decisions. Quoting from Prof. Dr Tarcisius Chin in an article on *Living longer, healthier and happier*:

> Having sufficient rest and sleep is an important ingredient in making a more, happier you. This offers your mind and body the sanctuary from stress and turbulence of daily living. Everyone deserves moments of solitude and meditation to recharge. When the vagaries of daily living get you down, give yourself a break and seek solace in meditation, massage, aromatherapy, or other relaxation methods to get your body and mind recharged. Make time and energy to plan for leisure activities as you would plan your workday.

> Having good physical health is also important. A healthy body makes for a healthy mind. Human beings are meant to walk,

to move about and to burn calories. The curse of modern day living is that we become victims of technology. Exercising regularly makes for a healthier you. Today most modern organizations have the latest technology employed to ease the work of their people. The downside of this is that it makes people become too sedentary in their lifestyle. You have to create the habit of moving about every half hour. There is no excuse not to exercise since you can exercise anywhere and at any-time. Taking the stairs rather than the lift, doing sit-ups and stretching your hands and back, walking to a colleagues table rather than sending him emails or even planning the day with a balance of paperwork and physical supervision to your work areas will enable you to move around. There are three purposes of exercise. One is aerobic-to keep the circulatory system in good condition. The second is strength; as we age our muscles and bones deteriorate and we need to exercise to operate at efficient levels. The third is flexibility and balance. Another important area to focus on is in the way we breathe. We are born to breathe using our full lung capacities as babies. Somehow we have become lazy and lapsed into shallow breathing. The purpose of breathing is to oxygenate the trillions of cells that make up our body. Therefore doing breathing exercises to improve our breathing so that all our blood cells will be fully nourished is important to our well being and good health. Make exercise habitual and regular and encourage your working colleagues and family members to also do so.

By being a more happier and balanced person, you will also not become attached to bad habits. Modern life with its high stress has pushed many individuals to take up bad habits such as smoking, excessive drinking, substance abuse and a life of indulgence and is reducing our life span and causing sudden death at our work places. Stay away from such bad habits. Biologically we are programmed to live to 120 years. Though with medical advances in detecting the likelihood of diseases, we can live to the eighties with medication, but illnesses once it comes will negatively impact the quality of life and become a burden to you, your family and organization as a whole. Going for regular health screening tests and check-ups will help to arrest medical problems before they become too serious. As the saying goes, "an ounce of prevention is better than a ton of cure".

> Stay away from junk food loaded with fats, salt and sugar and sugary and carbonated drinks. Substitute this with fresh fruits, fish, lean meat, nuts and vegetables   and green tea. These will help maintain body weight and increase anti-oxidants within your body. Eat like a king in the morning, a prince in the afternoon and a pauper at night. Alas, most of us do the exact opposite leading to obesity, bad dreams and disturbed sleep. You are what you eat. So follow the wise saying, "Eat to live, don't live to eat." Hence make it a point to practice these habits and have a work-life balance. You will be a much happier and healthier person.

When you learn how to also have a good time you will also not take yourself too seriously. Many successful executives, struggle all their lives to reach the top and achieve success and money and then realize that they now feel an emptiness inside. They miss the good times when they did things together with their spouse, family and friends. Those were the struggling years but they were the good years doing things together. Material wealth alone is not enough to give you happiness in life.

A happy person is one who also has a passion to pursue. We cannot be truly happy if we are not passionate over something. Having a passion will stimulate you and produce new challenges and make us happier in our work. Learning to play the guitar, learning to dance together with your spouse, making models of ships and aircraft, reading, gardening or doing community service. The important thing is to find an activity that will continue to give us pleasure and fulfillment.

A clown in a shopping mall was making ballons and giving them out to a bunch of excited children. The children were laughing gleefully at his antics and happy to be around him. There were also some happy adults who also asked for ballons. They still had the child in them, and why not? The clown was a middle aged gentleman who was holding a Bachelors and Masters degree from a renowned university and a working executive. When asked, he just said that this was a part-time position and that he did it because he loved to see people happy. That was his passion.

Finally be yourself. William James, the noted philosopher and psychologist, said: "Most people live, whether physically, intellectually or morally, in a very restricted circle of their potential." There are many people who go through life complaining that they have not been given the chance to succeed, never venturing to explore and use their treasures. The only way to reach anywhere is to start from where you are. Hence evaluate the potentials you have and develop them. The doubts, fears and anxieties of life should not overwhelm you. Accept who you are. Don't even try to imitate someone else.

LEAVE YOUR WORK BEHIND
& ENJOY YOUR HOLIDAY..!
ZZZZ
RING!
RONNIE

CHAPTER 4-
DETERMINATION TO OVERCOME CHALLENGES

"Mistakes are good, as long as you learn from them"

As a project manager, I am always called upon to deal with challenges. Every day has its own set of challenges to be dealt with. However the most difficult challenges do not arise from technical issues but those dealing with people. When such challenges crop up, everybody has a plan to fix it, but it takes a leader of real understanding to straighten things out. Most do not sort themselves out by leaving them alone. They usually get worse. Hence the sooner you deal with a problem the easier it is to fix it. A leader has to deal with such challenges decisively. Whether at work or in the family, a leader needs to know the 'pulse' of his people and nip problems in the bud before they can take root and become too big to manage. He must have the determination to overcome.

An effective way to keep close to the pulse of your people is to always engage or keep engaging with them. Whether it is be your children, your spouse or working colleagues, you need to always go down to the ground and listen to their feedback. You need to be accessible and visible. A healthy daily walk to the work site or to the shop floor and meeting with the workers and asking about the work progress will do a great deal to help a leader to understand and keep in touch with his fellow employees. Taking a walk with your children to the playground and listening to them talk about school and their friends. Sitting together with your spouse and having a quiet moment together and asking how the day went. All these will go a long way to maintaining the peace and harmony within your workplace and in your family at home.

As part of the team for a deep water large tension leg platform (TLP) which the company was building, I was asked to lead a team to trouble shoot on the reasons for the very high weld repair rates by the welders employed on the project. Deep water TLPs are huge floating oil platforms or floating production systems which are stationed in seas having great depths. They are moored to the sea floor by tendons which are part of an intricate mooring system which keeps the TLP in place. Senior Management was of the view that all such welders with high well repair rates should be immediately replaced with new ones as a solution to rectify the problem. However newly qualified welders employed to replace those rejected, also faced the same situation. The progress was being severely affected and it was becoming difficult to employ more welders. We needed to find out what was causing this high weld repair rates quickly.

We immediately organized a 1 day welder's forum to brainstorm on the reasons for the problem. All rejected welders were also invited to provide feedback. Almost all welders were unanimous in saying that it was due to defective welding machines and not due to lack of skills in welding. The Facilities Department, in charge of providing and maintaining the welding machines, however rejected this allegation, saying that all the machines were brand new and rented from our regular and well known suppliers.

After having the forum, we decided to go out into the field and check the information ourselves. The quality control department found that all the welding machines were in good order. Still not satisfied, and since we still had not identified the root cause of the problem, I decided to check a few of the machines personally together with my team. During the forum, many welders had complained that there was fluctuating currents emanating from the welding machines that had affected their welding quality. We finally discovered that though the welding machines were new units, the power sources supplying the current were provided by older, company owned, machines which were the source of the problem. Many of these machines were providing fluctuating currents. Hence replacing all power source machines resolved the issue once and for all. It was found that other projects were also facing the same situation and the benefit from this exercise was passed over to them too.

Many a time the easiest way is to blame the people. Hence we brought back all rejected welders and put them back on the job. Welding quality, progress and morale improved greatly thereafter. This was a good lesson learnt by the senior management who were too quick to blame the people rather than first investigating and finding out the root cause of the problem. It was also a lesson to respective departmental heads to go out into the field more regularly so as to be in touch with the reality of the situation on the ground.

Effective leaders deal with such challenges in their lives for the good of the people, the family and the organization. They always keep their finger on the 'pulse' of their people. Facing challenges takes courage and determination. It can also be a very exhilarating and rewarding experience when we go through difficulties and successfully overcome such challenges.

If you observe the birth of bees, you'll see that they emerge from their cells only after considerable struggle. Their hard efforts make their body fluids flow and this makes their muscles and wings gather strength and vitality. Deprived of this struggle, the bees will become incapable of fluttering their tender wings and fall to their deaths.

Stresses, temptations, difficulties, tensions, confrontations and struggles are part of life that toughen and strengthen us. When you are able to meet them squarely, they strengthen and develop your abilities, help you live creatively and makes you understand and be sensitive to other people. Facing challenges in life and at the workplace and combating them gives you confidence to attempt bigger things and bigger projects.

When George Mallory, was asked why he attempted to conquer the highest peak in the world, Everest, he answered, "Because it is there!". However the Nepali sherpa's who guide climbers up the mountain prefer to be a friend to Everest rather than try to conquer it. They believe that you should not try to conquer a friend rather you should become one with him. Helen Keller who was deaf and blind and relied completely on her sense of touch, wrote, "The marvelous richness of human experience would lose something of rewarding joy if there were no limitations to overcome. The hilltop hour would not be so wonderful if there were no dark valleys to traverse." She packed her life with amazing experiences. She wielded her handicap into her success. "Troubles are often the tools by which God fashions us for better things." (H.W.Beecher).

There are many men and women, who though born deformed, have not given up. The Malaysian, Mouth and Foot Painting Artists Association is run by artists who were born deformed but who want-not pity-but a chance to earn a living. Artists born with deformed hands use their foot to draw and paint. Likewise there are other men and women, who though born deformed, have not given up. They have overcome their adversities and converted them into their strength. The members have learned to draw and paint with the brush held in the mouth or with the toes and have all been deprived of the use of their hands by illness, injury or due to birth defects. We all have our own limitations or handicaps. If you cannot remedy your defects, then learn to accept and live with them, not grudgingly but joyfully. Discover your strengths and excel in them. Adversity when accepted willingly, brings out what is best in you. If you don't let go of the past, it will have a way of spoiling your present and prevent you from having a beautiful future. We all need an Everest to face to bring out the best in us!.

MT. CHALLENGE
RONNIE.

CHAPTER 5-ENTHUSIASM

"Enthusiasm, the spearhead of success"

"Enthusiasm moves the world" wrote A.J. Balfour a former British Prime Minister. An enthusiastic person is not only convinced that his purpose in life is worthwhile but he will leave no stone unturned to see that he achieves his goal. There is a deep sense of commitment and eagerness in work. Teresa Anne in her book Tips for Teens wrote:

"When persons are filled with zeal and hard work for a cause, such as the upliftment of the poor, the rehabilitation of lepers, liberating child-labourers, there emerge great saints like Mother Teresa." As a leader in an organization, you need to be able to transmit your enthusiasm to your fellow colleagues and employees alike. If you don't believe in your work, how can you then make others believe in what you are saying to them. Enthusiasm must be infectious so that people around you will respond to you positively. An enthusiastic leader will project eagerness and commitment providing that feeling of assurance that they are sincere in what they are saying. The best way to get the team excited is to be excited yourself. Whether it's on a project or an idea within the company, be excited about it and express confidence in your ability to achieve it. Have a clear goal and channel all your energy in a disciplined and focused manner. Aim high to reach your goal. Next, don't look back. Tenacity of purpose is extremely essential for success. "He is victorious who has constancy of purpose."

The famous American poet and philosopher, Ralph Waldo Emerson has defined thus, "Every great commanding movement in the annals of the world is the triumph of some enthusiasm. Nothing great was ever achieved without it." Taking modified excerpts from B.H. Liddell Hart's classic book *History Of The Second World War* the following is an account of the enthusiasm of one particular American General which turned the tide for the allies in Sicily.

During the second world war, the American General George S.Patton Jr commanding the US 7th Army was tasked with providing flanking support to the British 8th Army under General Montgomery in the Sicilian Campaign. The key to the Sicilian campaign was the town of Messina located at the north-eastern tip of the island and guarding the straits of Messina. Messina was the key for the allied re-entry into Europe via the toe of the Italian peninsula. As the British moved up the Sicilian Island along the eastern coastal road, they succeeded after three days' of stiff fighting in reopening the way into the plain of Catania but thereafter blocked by the tough terrain and the strong resistance from German reserves. Patton, always the tenacious commander, was brought in to put into action a new plan for the US 7th Army, from its original action of being a shield to the flank of the Eight Army's intended decisive drive for Messina and act also as a distraction to the enemy's concentration, into that of an offensive action and become the main spearhead.

Patton devised a plan to attempt three small amphibious landings and captured Palermo on the north-western part of the island and raced along the northern coastal road to Messina and liberated it before Montgomery.

It was Patton's enthusiasm and tenacity of purpose in believing that using amphibious outflanking moves would save the Sicilian campaign, and it did. If only the allies had used more of this, they could have cut off and captured most of the enemy. This could have shortened the Italian Campaign, since until the close of the Sicilian campaign and the successful escape of the four German divisions engaged there, the German defender of Italy, Field Marshal Kesselring, had only two German divisions to cover the whole of southern Italy. The allied armies could have easily rolled over the German defences and captured Italy and shortened the war.

Finally, Dale Carnegie in his book *The Leader in You* says, "You transmit enthusiasm through your eyes, in the way you move, the way you act all day, more than the way you write it in an email or memo".

All of us must have enthusiasm for something in life. It is what drives us and gets us up every day in the morning. You need to have an intense desire to succeed in your goals. The stronger the desire, the more powerful the inner force to fulfill that desire and the easier it will be to overcome any hurdles in the way to achieving success. Being passionate, motivated and enthusiastic for what you do every day has a powerful impact on those around you. So be enthusiastic.

SENIOR CITIZENS
CLUB.
RONNIE

CHAPTER 6-
RESPECT OTHERS

"You don't lose anything by being nice"

A young priest was celebrating Mass in church one Sunday morning, when the mobile phone of a particular elderly lady in the congregation, started ringing. Not only that, she proceeded to take the call and speak loudly to the other person on the phone. The priest however, stopped his homily and waited patiently for the lady to finish her call before proceeding to continue with the mass. Did he chide and scold her in front of the congregation. No, he did nothing of the sort. He showed great restraint and patience in handling the situation. Maybe it could have been something urgent. He respected the dignity of the lady. He waited until mass was over before he took her aside to talk to her. He respected her dignity and spoke to her in a way where she would be receptive. He didn't take the high ground and chide her from the pulpit. He treated his congregation in a most compassionate and respectful manner.

My wife has always something nice and respectful to say to the waitresses or sales persons whenever we go out to dine at a restaurant or buy groceries at a supermarket. I have never seen a time when a simple thank you or a pleasant greeting was missing no matter in what mood she is in irrespective of the culture, ethnicity or background of the people she greeted. There would always be a pleasant smile and something nice to say to them. She knows the power of respecting the dignity of others and in return she is served well wherever she goes and the people who serve her do so with a glow and a smile on their faces. People want to be treated and recognized as individuals because we're all human beings. What's important is the way in which people are treated on a daily basis. A pleasant smile, a simple thank you or a good morning greeting does go a long way in creating a warm and pleasant environment.

As a project manager, my day would always start with a daily morning safety briefing at the work site, and spending the first two hours of the morning, walking around the work sites. Meeting and greeting the people at the site was something we did as part of our work culture. Stopping to speak to people, giving them a friendly wave, giving someone a piece of safety advise whenever observing an unsafe condition or unsafe act, giving little safety tokens of appreciation to deserving workers, would go a long way in making the people at the work site, appreciate the concern and need to work safely. Do people respond to these small things? They most surely do and that was shown in the many successful projects completed, without any injuries or loss of life, in our company.

Treating someone with respect, remembering a name, giving encouragement to someone, just showing them that you are with them by walking in the hot sun and sweating it out with them and even climbing up the ladders to go up to the extreme ends to see them work safely–those are just the most important things any leader can do. These basics are what works. This is what separates you from the rest, by doing the simple things which count for people and doing it always. Don't just tell them, but show them by your actions that we are in this together.

In a certain educational institute, staff employed to man the front desk would always have to bear the ire of customers complaints pertaining to delays in getting their refunds due to the delay by the Finance Department in making such payments. Front desk staff would always follow up and notify the Finance Department on customers' feedback and their unhappiness in the unwarranted delays even though all documents were in order. However the Finance Manager, in charge of signing such cheques, would take such complaints lightly and purposely delay making the refund payments so as to improve on the company cash flow. She would however not try to explain to customers, who were made up of the parents of the students at the institute, on the reasons for the delays in making the refund payments. She would just avoid meeting the customers and let customers vent their anger on the poor front desk staff.

This same Finance Manager would however berate and shout at the same staff, when fees from students became due and not paid on the due date even though the same staff had given reminders as was required by the procedure. The staff would be blamed for not doing their job. Many of the affected staff tried to explain their situation to higher management but the situation did not improve, since the Finance Manager was a close friend of the owner of the institute and got away with the continued verbal abuse of staff.

The situation for these front desk staff became more and more stressful and intolerable, having to bear the brunt of such verbal abuse, and some of them started to fall ill. Staff morale and productivity suffered and with time many of them started to look for jobs, with a better working environment, in other organizations. In time many loyal, experienced and hardworking staff left the institute. This ultimately affected the institute's reputation and caused revenue to fall, since many prospective students shunned this institute and went to others.

You will see many similar cases in many different organizations irrespective of the type of industry you are in. You may also have experienced or are experiencing such a situation yourself. As a leader we need to treat employees like colleagues and not be condescending, dictating or berate them in any way. A real positive environment cannot be created that way.

So why do so many managers treat their employees in a demeaning manner and shout at the people who work for them? The problem lies in themselves and it is due to their own low self-esteem. They try to create an aura of strength when in actual fact they are not really tough managers. It is a cover to hide their own discomfort and low self-esteem.

Recognize the humanity that everyone in the organization shares. Pulling rank and playing the big boss doesn't motivate people to do anything. On the contrary people will do it out of resentment or fear. This will only create an unpleasant work environment and increase the stress levels and certainly reduce the overall productivity of people or even cause the loss of good and experienced employees who will leave at the first opportunity which comes their way.

Abusing people verbally and demanding respect by giving orders and creating an atmosphere of fear and toughness produces negative results. Intimidation only creates resentment from people. Managers who are condescending only create enemies within their own organizations and this could become disruptive and may even cause people to sabotage the work and work to rule. It is more effective to treat employees as human beings and treat them with dignity and respect.

As a leader be a mentor and treat people as equals. Most organizations have this saying- *"employees are our assets."* Don't just make this a by-line but make the employees believe what you say. Go down to the ground. Maintain a sense of humility. Always put yourself in the other person's shoes.

A good leader will challenge his employees to come out with good ideas for improvements. Encouraging employees to work together as a team and empowering them to plan the improvements by involving them and making them feel that they have the power to influence and make changes will create a very healthy and happy organization. Making people feel that they are important to the organization will motivate the organization to achieve its goals.

IF I DON'T GET A GOOD
SOLUTION BY THE END OF TODAY
I'LL SACK THE LOT OF YOU!
RONNIE

CHAPTER 7-
SALUTE TEAMWORK

Today's modern organizations cannot be run like the old organizations of yesteryears. Old organizations which followed the pyramid structures where the boss gives out the orders and the minions follow through and complete tasks can no longer work. As stated in the introduction chapter of this book, leaders can no longer just issue orders and expect employees to mindlessly obey. Personal relationships can no longer be just taken for granted. The leaders of this cultural revolution will have to establish a real vision and a sense of real values within organizations they wish to lead and manage conditions of almost constant change. Modern day organizations cannot be operated like armies. In today's modern organizations, we need to build teams, lead teams and have team players. The message to the whole organization must be-we either sink or swim together. Hence this concept of teamwork being the key ingredient in the success or failure in the organization must be made the culture of the organization.

Leaders must set the vision and mission of the organization, developing this vision and mission together with the employees.

Employees must be empowered to set the vision and mission statements together with the leadership so that there will be buy-in by all to achieve the goals set in the end of the day. A strong leader is required to focus on the implementation of that vision. The leader must be able to explain the vision, and set the goals to achieving that vision and make the team understand how their accomplishments will impact on the organization as a whole.

The leader, once the goals have been set, must appoint the goal champions for each of the goals to be achieved for the overall vision to be realized. The whole team has to work as one well-oiled machine to win. If one fails then the whole team fails. Goal champions will have to motivate their teams by being responsible for ensuring their team members work together and contribute their efforts to fit in with the goals.

People need to feel that their contributions are important. They must feel interested and devote their complete attention to the goals at hand. Team leaders must encourage active participation and come up with group decisions and not dictate solutions.

Project Managers, Product Managers, ship captains and even politicians will find that emphasizing on how everyone's contribution fits in together can get the project running successfully or the product launched into the market smoothly or to sail the ship through a bad storm or even winning an election together. When the team does well, the leader must also ensure that they are rewarded whether by praise or with bonuses or with a well deserved promotion. In the same way if the team fails then it's the responsibility of the leader to stand together and accept the greater portion of the blame. Only then can the team build up confidence and believe in their leader. A good leader believes in his team and the team in return will reciprocate that belief.

Leaders must also be able to identify each team member's individual talents and personalities and use them to the advantage of the team and organization as a whole. Today's modern organizations employ psychological based tools to identify the different personalities of their employees such as the FIRO-B Instrument, first developed in the late 1950's, is now one of the most widely used tools for helping people better understand themselves and how they can work more effectively with others especially in areas such as team building and development. The Myers-Briggs Type indicator (MBTI) personality assessment tools however is used to describe the personality preferences derived from the answers to the assessment instrument. The MBTI instrument is not a measure of skills or abilities in any area but rather, employees within each team will get an insight to help become aware of each other's particular style and to better understand and appreciate the helpful ways that people differ from one another.

Another tool commonly employed is the Margerison-McCann Team management profiling systems. The team management profile questionnaire does not measure skill or experience where an employee may have good abilities in areas of work where they may have low preferences. However, where there is a good match between preferences and the demands of the job, there may be a better likelihood to enjoy work, develop skills and perform well. Where a group is made up of individuals with complementary work preferences, the team has a greater chance of being effective. Hence the leader is responsible to identify the different personalities, preferences and aptitude and develop and strengthen the people in the team and be also responsible for the lives and long term careers of the people in the team. The leader has to ask team members how they can improve, what sort of new responsibilities that they would like to take, where they wish to go in their career and to use this knowledge and experiences within the team to help the team members achieve their goals. There are many other similar techniques and tools being employed today.

As a project manager I have had the great opportunity to work on several oil and gas fabrication projects for my company.

In a career spanning close to thirty years, I have seen the transformation of the organization which I worked for, from the rigid pyramid organization system, to modern day organization teams. In the early days, the main criterion for success was the achievement of the profit margins of the company. There would be no stress on team building sessions nor identifying the team member's strengths and weaknesses or their aptitude or preference. Project teams will be appointed based on the project requirement and as per trade, experience and availability of the people within the company. The boss will direct the whole show and the rest of his minions will carry out the work as directed. This worked well as long as the work was manageable but as work became more and more complex and work standards and specifications from customers grew wider and bigger and more demanding, competition became more intense with more players coming into the market, costs started escalating whilst at the same time margins needed to be lowered to remain in competition. Oil prices began to fluctuate and we were also at this period in time, hit by the cyclical economic downtrends and the Asian Financial crisis. It became important to get the right people for the right jobs working within teams and team based organizations started to be nurtured. It did not happen easily since to break the shackles of the old pyramid structure was painful and saw the demise of many in the old organization structure. Team building became a culture within the organization and project teams worked closely between themselves and other team members and customers.

Larger and more complex projects were being managed better and completed successfully. The organization grew and became the company of choice for various customers. This phenomenal success was due directly to the team based organizations within and the values nurtured by employees who stuck together in difficult times and enjoyed the fruits of their labour during the good times.

MANY `ANTS` MAKE LIGHT WORK !

CHAPTER 8-

HAVING DISCIPLINE AND FOCUS

"Never, ever, ever, ever give up!"

In a manufacturing plant in the southern state of Johor, Malaysia, a 1,500 tonne structure, the height of a 15 storey building was being moved to its load-out point beside the jetty to be lifted onto an ocean going barge. The structure was being moved by a self-propelled modular transporter/trailer (SPMT) which is a platform vehicle which has a large array of wheels and is remotely controlled. Suddenly, there was a loud crack. One of the two transverse beams on which the structure was being supported on, had failed under the strain of the weight and vibration caused by the movement. It was by a miracle that the tall structure did not collapse to the ground. The structure was now tilting at a precarious angle and it was by a miracle that it had not fallen, ...but for how long?

What made the difference that evening and helped to avert a disaster from occurring and saved the reputation of the company, was the ability of its leaders to galvanize everyone. All other work was put on hold and complete focus was to be on the task of getting the unstable structure back onto an even keel. The leaders immediately formed an emergency task force made up of all the experienced and key personnel within the organization, who worked together to come up with the best possible solution. A plan was prepared and approved after calculated engineering analysis had been carried out. All heavy lifting equipment and manpower required for the operation was mobilized within a few hours. Leave for all management and essential personnel was also cancelled. All non-essential personnel were requested to go home due to the danger posed by the unstable structure if it did collapse to the ground. A collapse could cause a potential minor tremor in the ground which could shake and damage all surrounding buildings. The work to have the structure back onto a safe footing and complete the load out process within the schedule was done without any further mishap and completed over a 24 hour period without wasting a single moment.

The customer, though alarmed by the situation, was however very impressed with the emergency response taken to rectify a potentially dangerous situation. They saw how the people in the organisation acted with discipline and focus and worked hard as a team in getting the job completed under extremely stressful and difficult odds. They saw that the leaders within the organization never lost their focus and had kept their eyes on the Big picture. There was no sign of any panic by either the leadership nor its people. Not only had a disaster been averted, but the reputation of the company and its people had also been saved. They never gave up. An adversity had been turned into a success and a good learning experience.

Staying focused and having self discipline is the recipe and makes the difference between success and failure. Success needs hard work. You need to believe in yourself and have the fortitude and be persistent and not be distracted in order to achieve your goals which you have set in your mind. This recipe works whether in a business organization, or in your own family. Winston Churchill, told the house of commons in his first speech as prime minister:

"We have before us many, many long months of struggle and of suffering. I've nothing to offer but blood, toil, tears and sweat. You ask, what is our policy? I can say it is to wage war, by sea, land and air with all our might, and with all the strength that God can give us, to wage war against a monstrous tyranny, never surpassed in the dark, lamentable catalogue of human history. That is our policy. You ask, what is our aim? I can answer in one word: It is victory, victory at all costs, and victory in spite of terror, however long and hard the road may be; for without victory, there is no survival."

In 1941, during England's most difficult days, Churchill returned to his old school Harrow, to give a commencement address. Churchill made his way to the podium, stared out over the assemblage of boys, and gave his commencement message :

" This is the lesson : never give in, never give in, never, never, never, never - in nothing, great or small, large or petty - never give in except to convictions of honour and good sense. Never yield to force, never yield to the apparently overwhelming might of the enemy."

Churchill galvanized the British people to stand united and disciplined and remain focused on achieving final victory throughout the difficult war years. They stayed united and succeeded even though going from failure to failure without loss of enthusiasm. A good leader will remain focused and be disciplined, working hard to achieve the goals set and be able to galvanize the people to also do the same. To never give up is the policy of most of the successful people. To have the added discipline to follow up on every detail of your work every time is what makes such people very valuable assets to any company. If your boss and colleagues know that you can be trusted to do the job and follow through till successful completion then you are on the path to success. Following up whether it is in the many details of a work process, or in calling to reconfirm on an appointment, or checking the route to an important meeting so that you will be on time, these are the traits of successful people.

NEVER, NEVER, NEVER, EVER GIVE IN...!
OCCUPIED EUROPE
BRITAIN STANDS ALONE
RONNIE.

CHAPTER 9-INTEREST

"The hallmark of a great leader: Humility"

As a leader whether in the work place or at home with your spouse or with your children, showing interest builds closeness, unity and confidence in the people around you. Keeping aside time for the people you work with and the people whom you care for is what makes for a harmonious and united workplace and family. We need to touch base and know the 'pulse' of the people around us. Dale Carnegie in The Leader in You reiterates a very important fact about human psychology:

> One of the most basic facts of human psychology is the fact that we feel nice and flattered when other people shower attention on us. We feel special and important. We are attracted to people who show interest in us and who want to know us better. The feeling becomes mutual and we start to give the same back to them. We want to know them better and become good friends in the process. People respond to people who show sincere interest in them. Displays of interest are the fundamental building blocks of good human relationship.

As a father and a husband, coming home daily to your family and giving your spouse and your children a little time before the end of the day is important in giving them the feeling of being special and important. Showing interest in their day and helping with the dishes or the children with their homework or school project are the things which show that you care. We should not be so busy that we have no time for the people around us. It is the people around us who make us who we are. Good leaders show interest. They will always meet and greet their people on a regular basis.

Walking the shop floor at a regular time and talking to the people. Holding weekly and monthly meetings so that everyone knows that there is a scheduled time where they can voice their concerns or ideas or anything that they feel is important to them will show that you, as their leader, care for and are concerned about their feelings and willing to show sincere interest in them.

As a leader be approachable, friendly and caring to your people and be interested in them and their families. By not forgetting the importance of the roles played by everyone from the receptionist, clerks, technicians and others you'll be surprised how much quicker productivity will improve in your work place. Human beings will respond immediately to sincere expressions of warmth.

Whether at work or at home with the family, have a little fun. Organize fun time at the workplace such as celebrating birthdays or having an in house competition and handing out prizes to those who win. Have a monthly team lunch together with everyone. Take the children to the park and play fun games with them. Take your spouse out for dinner or watch a movie together. These are the ways of saying I care about you. It will be fun. It will make you feel good about yourself.

It will help develop your relationship, gain self confidence and make your life and the lives of others happier.Itcan be as simple as greeting someone whether in person or over the phone in a pleasant and warm voice which will make anyone feel that you are expressing genuine interest in them, making them feel welcome and happy.

Leading can also be very painful, but this is part of the job. Pain causes humility and humility makes you humble and humbleness is the mark of all great leaders who show genuine interest for the welfare of their people.

DON'T BE TOO HARD ON OUR DIRECTORS. MANY OF THEM ARE DOING THE WORK OF THREE MEN..... THE THREE STOOGES....!
HUMP..F!
RONNIE

CHAPTER 10-
POSITIVE MINDSET

"You will become what you think you will be"

Our minds can create thoughts which affect our lives in more ways than we know. What happens next depends on how we react to situations. How we react again depends on how we think. If we think positively, our reactions will also be positive. If we think negatively, then our reactions will also be negative. Khalil Gibran said, "Your living is determined not so much by what life brings to you as by the attitude you bring to life; not so much by what happens to you as by the way your mind looks at what happens." God has given everyone all that he or she needs to be joyful. Life is meant to be happy.

There is a children's tale about a little fish and a bigger fish. "Life here is so dull, the same water, the same old companions, the same kind of food day after day... I think the other rivers must be exciting." "I'm not quite sure", responded the older fish thoughtfully, "Here we have plenty of friends, no shortage of food, neither any lack of water." Without heeding this wise advice, the smaller fish swam to the river bank and was thrilled to see a large pond nearby. She jumped out of the water, without a second thought and landed directly into the jaws of a huge fish.

Be happy with what you have and don't lose your happiness by always comparing with others. The grass is not always green on the other side. A study on the happiness quotient of people around the world showed that the happiest people were found, not in the world's richest countries, but in poorer regions. Though they lived a hard life, they were happy and grateful for what they had. They had a positive mindset about themselves.

Cognitive Behavior Therapy (CBT) developed by Dr. Aaron T. Beck at the University of Pennsylvania in the 1960's, is based on a cognitive theory of psychopathology. The cognitive model describes how people's perceptions of, or spontaneous thoughts about, situations influence their emotional behavioral (and often physiological) reactions. By learning to identify and evaluate your "automatic thoughts" (spontaneously occurring verbal or imaginary cognitions), and to correct your thinking so that it will resemble reality, your distress usually decreases, and you will be able to behave more functionally.

Think positively by having the right attitude. Count your blessings rather than counting what you don't have. Recondition your thoughts to identify and correct your attitudes. Since attitudes are the result of repeated thinking. Thinking is nothing but talking that goes on in your mind. So listen carefully to yourself and change negative attitudes to positive ones.

We live in a world today that is interconnected and hardwired. Everyone is able to gain access to information and data in a real time situation using our palm held iphones or handheld personal computers at anytime and day. All this information which is bombarding us can have either a positive or a negative impact. These outside influences will try to change our thought process. Having a strong positive mental attitude will help us to remain positive at all times even when faced with unexpected situations which can strike us at anytime. Expect the unexpected. Remind yourself that, change is the only constant. Contrary to what people believe, what makes you happy is in the way you handle a situation. External situations and influences are not what make a person unhappy. It is how you take it and handle it. It is how we react to those situations and outside influences, whether they are good or bad, that makes the difference. Hence your happiness is in your own hands.

Since the only certainty in life is uncertainty, we must ensure that we are always ready to accept the unexpected. Once we have trained our minds to accept this, we must now look for ways and means to overcome it, no matter how serious or difficult it may be. Train your mind to develop this positive outlook. Every day the moment we wake up, push out all negative thoughts and control your thought process to always think happy and good thoughts. You only have today, so why not enjoy it rather than spoiling the day. Control your thought process. Our mental attitude comes from the power of our mind which can change our lives. Think happy and you will be happy, think success and you will succeed, think healthy and you will be healthy. Happiness is not in anything, in any place or in any person. It is in your correct attitude.

The guest speaker at a charity dinner was a highly acclaimed cancer specialist. He was one of the patrons for an organization which assisted cancer patients who were undergoing treatment at the specialist hospital's oncology department that he headed. After running through all his slides showing the various types of cancers and their treatment, he admitted that medical science had no conclusive answers as to what caused cancer in a human body. He said that intense stress and anxiety has a serious impact on our mental health and this can have an impact on the cells in our bodies. Hence the advice given by this highly qualified and experienced oncologist was to remain positive at all times. This is the power we hold in our minds.

A good way to remain positive and push out negativity in our lives is by humour. Humour is vital in making us happy. Laugh your worries away. There are so many things which can irritate, worry or annoy you. Be like a duck. Let the negative thoughts run over you like water running over a duck's body. Don't let them enter your mind. Push them out or even better, stop them from entering in. Positive thoughts not only make you self-confident but it also rubs off on others. The aura of positivity draws people to you. Refrain from mixing with negative thinking people. They will sap your energy. In organizations, a leader has to fight hard against those "energy sappers" and instill positive feelings and attitudes. One bad apple will ultimately spoil the whole basket of fruits and can lead to the failure of an organization. The rot starts one step at a time.

Road rage occurs when one driver becomes angry with another and reacts in a violent manner to the other. However if such drivers could develop the right kind of attitude by thinking positively and say to themselves "Never mind, I am not going to get angry and shorten my life. The other guy isn't going to get far either, so let's just switch on the radio and enjoy some music." There's not much you can do by fretting and being angry in a bad situation. You will then be a much happier and healthier person.

Marcus Aurelius said, "The universe is change; our life is what our thoughts make it." So happy thoughts makes for a happy life. So practice constantly your thoughts. Start the day by keeping only good thoughts. End the day by thinking happy thoughts. Thank God for the beautiful day and for the gift of another day. Yesterday's just a memory and tomorrow but a dream. You have only today. So stay positive and be happy!

THE GRASS IS NOT ALWAYS GREEN ON THE OTHER SIDE
NOOO...O!
AAH...DINNER!
RONNIE

CHAPTER 11-
ACT, DON'T REACT

"Genius is to know when to act"

As a father, I always do my best to give a good example to my children. Believe me when I say that children, from a very young age have memories which they take to adulthood. Sometimes, as a parent, in the midst of juggling between, work, family and yourself, you tend to forget that your little children also have feelings and hurt easily. During a visit by a relative, a young boy got into a fight with his young cousin who was of the same age. To maintain the peace, the boy's father called his son over and gave him a smack on the wrist, and told him not to fight with his cousin based on his aunt's hearsay of who started the fight. Though his father soon forgot about this little incident, the boy's little heart had been deeply
hurt and this incident was etched in his mind, to resurface much later in life during his adulthood. The father, who had been his hero, had not stood up for him. We all have something similar etched in our childhood memories within us. Leadership, like parenting can be painful since we are not perfect beings. We all make mistakes. The important lesson is that we learn from them.

In any organization, there will always be individuals who are prone to spreading rumours and listening to gossip and causing discord. The same occurs within families too. Good leaders never act on mere hearsay, they first obtain all the facts and then follow through with the next course of action. By doing so, they instill confidence in their employees who will feel that they have a just leader above them who is fair and honest in leading them. First, go to the persons involved and listen to them. Obtain all the facts of the matter. Analyse what course of action would need to be taken. Then act on them.

Most people who react to every situation generally have a poor self-image of themselves. There is a beautiful prayer called The Serenity Prayer written by the American theologian Reinhold Niebuhr (1892-
1971). Quoting From the best-known Form: 'God grant me the serenity to accept the things I cannot change, Courage to change the things I can, And the wisdom to know the difference.'

No human being is created perfect, so don't expect perfection in yourself or from others. As leaders we need to be aware of the forces around us which damage our positive self-esteem leading to a poor self-image of ourselves. Focus your energy on your strengths and be proud of your achievements and your own personal qualities. Always picture a positive image of yourself and keep this afresh in your mind and appreciate it. Never try to please everyone. Be true to yourself and be just yourself. When people who know little about you say negative things about you, challenge them! If others look upon you as "inferior" you slowly interiorize it, developing a poor self-image and start behaving with inferiority. However when someone thinks highly of us and put great faith in our abilities, we tend to fulfill their expectations by calling forth hidden resources within us.

Hence don't allow self-doubt to sap your mental energy. Assert yourself and let others know how you feel and who you really are. Unless they know you, they really cannot appreciate you. Expressing yourself firmly will make you respected and taken seriously. Take interest in others so others will also take interest to get to know you better. Get feedback from people who know you well and work on your weaknesses whilst at the same time nurturing your strengths.

Learn to understand your fears and work to overcome them. Worry and anxiety within us comes from the unknown fears of the future. Your fears say something about yourself. Listen to them. The only way to free yourself from them is to confront the very things you are afraid of. If you are afraid to speak in front of a crowd, practice by speaking up in small groups. Gradually you will build your confidence to address bigger groups and become an effective speaker.

Finally a good leader is also a good friend to himself. Unless you love yourself first, you cannot love others. Don't be too hard on yourself and take care of yourself. Look upon yourself as an important person deserving your own self-esteem. Have faith in yourself, accepting, trusting and being friendly with yourself. Enjoy and relish all your good memories and treasure them and relive them so that you can relive the present moment more fully and appreciatively. Start the day and end it with a prayer by glorifying God with a grateful heart for all the good things and blessings which comes from him.

I WILL GET BACK INTO
SHAPE....
I CAN DO IT! ...
Ronnie

CHAPTER 12-
CARING FOR OTHERS

"You are only as useless as you think you are"

As a project manager, I had to deal with the many technical and commercial aspects of successfully managing a project. However the most important part of the success was always the safety of the people on the job. To complete a project safely and without any accidents was also the top priority and the target to achieve. We would always speak about and think about achieving a zero loss time accident target. Every project team's key performance indicator would be tied to this target. During our daily safety walks we would pick up unsafe acts and unsafe conditions at the work site. Daily safety talks would always be on the subject of working safely and going home to our families without injuries.

Meeting and greeting the people working at the sites was made a regular affair. Making it a point to talk to at least two workers at the site daily and talking to them about their work and problems faced was part of our project management culture. Showing the people working at the work site that we respected their hard work and that we cared for their safety created a conducive environment. It was not just about completing the project on time, within budget, and with highest quality, but about getting it done with no injuries because the people are the most important part of the project. To show them that we cared for them and their families was the single most important thing that led to the safe and successful completion of projects.

Humility needs to be nurtured if one yearns to be a caring person. A good leader is one who shows his caring nature by the way he talks and by the way he treats his people. In ancient China there lived a wise old man. Lao-Tzu said, "What have the river and sea done to be kings of the hundred valleys? They put themselves below them and that is why they reign in the hundred valleys. If the Saint wants to be at the top of his people, he first has to learn how to talk with humility. If he wants to lead his people, he should be last. That is how the saint is at the top of his people and he doesn't make them suffer. Willingly they place him at the top and do not get tired of him, since he doesn't compete with anybody, nobody can compete with him."

In the family, showing care and concern to your spouse and children would create a positive home environment. Not just saying it but also doing the little stuff such as helping to clean the house, washing the dishes, taking care of those who are sick in the family will motivate members to work in harmony together knowing that their feelings and physical wellbeing was being taken care of. When a child comes home and shows his report card. Do we compare it with the best results in the class and just focus on the A's, or do we focus on those areas where they have shown good results and encourage them to do better? Give praise on those good achievements and then show them the other areas which need improvement. Caring means always giving encouragement and motivation. Your children will then work harder to achieve better results the next time.

In many businesses, the role of the warehouse is often underestimated. The underestimation of this vital element in the

Supply Chain Process often leads to poor morale within the people working in the warehouse. Failure to acknowledge the skills and equipment required to operate today's warehouses, which are called on to handle varied types and larger volumes of goods and services, in addition to doing it faster and with no errors, is now causing many warehouses to fail and needing expensive rectification and consultant costs.

As a Senior Supply Chain Manager, I would always face a very difficult time trying to convince management whenever it came to employing the right skills for the various differing requirements within the warehouse. Management would always use the warehouse as a form of dumping ground for underperforming employees from other departments. Managing a warehouse, to top management was not thought to be on the same level of difficulty as managing say, the Engineering department.

A young engineer, who had been 'discarded' by another department was one such individual who was transferred to the warehouse. I had never seen a more
dejected looking individual. He knew that his transfer was intentional and that management was indirectly giving a subtle message to him to either perform or leave. It was an unspoken ultimatum and he knew it. I immediately scheduled a meeting with him. First step was to listen to what he had to say. Listening was the best way to learn to know him. During the breaks in the conversation, I asked him questions on things he had raised especially on why he thought he had performed poorly in his former department. After giving him his time to open out his thoughts, I finally made it clear that as far as I was concerned, I was wiping the slate clean and offering him a new beginning to start afresh in a new job scope and in an entirely new environment. Was he interested? You bet he was!

Our conversation now grew to how he could help to improve the warehouse processes. This young engineer used his talents to improve the online warehouse processes and train the other operators to better perform and improve internal productivity. In the two years he stayed with the warehouse, he became a key element in the development and implementation of improvements for the various warehousing systems. He became a vital part of the team and felt a sense of belonging and ownership. He now felt useful, and important. His self–esteem which had taken a severe beating was now back intact. This all happened due to a simple act of caring shown by someone who did not give up on him. By listening patiently and with an open mind and showing genuine care and concern for his future well-being and giving him encouragement to express his ideas fully, he was now a transformed person.

In 1948, the American sociologist Robert K. Merton coined the term "self-fulfilling prophecy" Merton's description of the self-fulfilling prophecy is rooted in the Thomas theorem, formulated by sociologists W. I. Thomas and D. S. Thomas. This theorem states that if people define situations as real, They are then real in their consequences. It reflects the fact that beliefs act as social power to shape our behaviors in very real ways.

We need to firmly believe that everyone is useful and have their own particular talent and skills and with the right attitude, interest and motivation, can be assimilated within the organization.A caring nature will motivate anyone to perform well even in an environment which may be new and alien to them.

Caring about others and motivating them can make them useful and productive. Giving them a second chance and treating them well, works. No one is useless, unless he is made to think he is.

WE NEED TO IMPROVE COMPANY MORALE, SO I'VE DECIDED TO APPROVE A BONUS FOR MYSELF THIS YEAR!

CHAPTER 13-TAKE RESPONSIBILITY

"...do to others as you would have them do to you"

A project I was involved in was awarded to the company by a Japanese client. It involved the procurement, construction, onshore pre-commissioning and load-out of an additional compressor module for an existing offshore oil and gas platform. This was the first job awarded by a Japanese Company and all specifications were in Japanese standard units. As the subcontractor's representative to the client, I realized in one of my site walks that an instruction from the client representative to remove an absolutely correctly installed beam was wrong. However he was adamant that he was right. So I issued the instruction to cut out the beam. A week later he came over to my office and requested that the removed beam be reinstalled back at the clients own cost. After which he bowed profoundly and apologized for his mistake and said that he alone will take full responsibility for this error. We did as he instructed but I informed our contracts engineer not to charge the client for this additional work even though we had incurred a fair bit of money in additional cost for this work.

As the project came to a successful close, this small gesture was returned tenfold when the client did not claim back for materials which they had a right to claim back for. I also learned that the Japanese consider the discovery of a mistake or error as a key towards further improvement. This is what makes many Japanese companies highly successful and we can do well to embrace this concept. You can't expect others to admit their mistakes when you are unwilling to expect the same from yourself. "Do unto others what you want others to do unto yourself", is the best way to get this message across to everyone in an organization. In the case of the Japanese client, he set the example. By readily admitting his fault and humbly apologizing, he set the stage to stop any blame game from happening which so often is the case in many other organizations, where rather that admitting fault there will be the regular finger pointing and witch hunts.

In human psychology we know that everyone has an inherent defense mechanism built within us. When we blame other people for something, they will almost immediately contradict us and deny it and start defending their actions. The truth is we all make mistakes. There is none among us who do not make mistakes. We are also very fast to point out other people's mistakes easily and criticize them for it. But when we make mistakes and are at the receiving end of it, we really hate it. We hate to admit our own mistakes and go to great lengths to justify our own actions. We don't like to be told we are wrong, or to receive a bad appraisal of our performance.

People who work in the service industry know this well. Providing service with a smile is a motto which goes a very long way to satisfying customers even when the customer can be wrong or difficult. To build customer or vendor relationships, be the first to admit your mistake. By readily admitting mistakes and apologizing quickly, you will see that the other person will soften and even reassure you that it's okay. It's true for all relationships whether in a company, family or with your friends and neighbours.

Hence in an organization, built on a platform knowing everyone is prone to making mistakes but what is important is to admit it readily and learn from it, such organizations encourage creativity and will grow to be stronger and better. If you are afraid to make mistakes, you will make nothing. No one can be right or successful all the time. A winner forges ahead learning from his mistakes. If you don't pick up courage and venture, nothing will be achieved. Confucius once said, "Our greatest glory is not in never failing, but in rising every time we fail."

Post-mortems are conducted within organizations when their projects have shown failure to achieve the set targets or have failed disastrously causing a painful dent in their bottom lines. Most failures can be seen to have taken place when the project leaders fail to take responsibility. There is a lack of transparency and the failure to admit fault ultimately leads to the failure of the project. 'A volcano does not erupt overnight. There are many signs which take place before the cataclysmic eruption.' A responsible leader will not take such signs lightly. He will take responsibility to admit the weaknesses and take steps to remedy them before they become more serious.

During the 1997-1999 Asian financial crisis, many organizations were left in a very difficult position. There was a great need to grow the business and increase shareholders returns at a time when new projects were getting scarce and margins becoming leaner. Though they had the cash they were pressured to increase their order books and some jobs were accepted even with zero profit margins. This was a nightmare for many of the project leaders since they were asked to manage and complete projects successfully with almost no margin for errors. Of course most projects failed in the one area which was cost and this ate into company cash balances. What did the leaders within such organizations do? Did they take responsibility for their actions which led to this failure? No. Many top leaders started apportioning the blame onto their project managers. They were protecting their own seats. Finger pointing at everybody else became the name of the game. However most post-mortem audits conducted, ultimately found that the company's top management was responsible for the losses. They had ignored all the warning signs and went ahead to accept projects at rock bottom prices just to provide a glowing picture to the share holders.

These very painful lessons were learnt by such organizations which lead to the creation of mandatory risk management for all projects before taking them on. If an organization or person knows how the mistakes happened, why it happened and what steps are needed to be taken so that they won't be repeated, then there will not be any necessity for anyone to point fingers or make anyone a 'scapegoat'. Think before you blame someone. Admit your own mistakes and take steps to not repeat them.

IT WASN'T ME...
RONNIE

CHAPTER 14-INTEGRITY

"you reap the harvest of what you sow and plant"

Bhopal (Madhya Pradesh), India
Population 900,000
Dec. 3rd 1984
0200 hrs

As the people living in the beautiful and peaceful Indian city of Bhopal, with its rich heritage and historical past, slept, a large storage tank containing deadly methyl isocyanate (MIC) at the city's Union Carbide India Limited's (UCIL) pesticide plant, started leaking deadly poisonous gas into the atmosphere. The gas cloud which formed should have dissipated away but due to the cold winter temperature of 2º Celsius, the gas cloud flowed down to ground level and moving with the prevailing wind direction, extinguished the lives of every single living thing in its path. Men, women, children and animals were killed or maimed along its path. It was later found that 43 tons of toxic MIC gas stored had actually been released, before the fault had been remedied. The plant siren started blaring only 2 hours later.

The next morning, dawned to scenes of utter desolation and misery. Emergency Response teams, many made up of volunteers, were shocked at the scenes at the affected areas. I was in one such group made up of volunteers from the engineering college where I was in my 4th year of undergraduate studies. There were many survivors blinded and struggling to breathe. Dead cattle and buffaloes were lying everywhere.

At the city's main hospital, the scene was of utter but organized chaos. The medical personnel were trying to cope with an unprecedented situation with hundreds upon hundreds of dead bodies and screaming survivors who were being brought in. Doctors conducting autopsies, were overwhelmed by the gas released from the lungs of corpses. The blood was seen to be pink in colour and not red due to oxygen depletion. This was how deadly this gas was. Vultures were circling in the air. At the children's ward there were hundreds of children of all ages, including babies as young as a few days old, all fighting for their lives. Many pregnant women aborted their babies due to the effect of the gas. Methyl isocyanate eats up the mucous membranes within the lungs and causes irreparable damage causing those affected to die a slow, painful and lingering death. The effect on the eyes is akin to rubbing chilli powder into your eyes causing excruciating pain.

This was the world's first and still is the world's worst man-made industrial disaster. The affects of this disaster are still being felt, though the world has largely forgotten about it. An estimated 16,000 lives were lost. However for over 500,000 people exposed directly or indirectly to the gas, the suffering and death still goes on for many of them to this day.

Mine is an eye witness account. Why have I added this account under this chapter on integrity? It is to narrate the story of how corruption and greed can destroy the lives of many and leave a legacy of misery. This was a preventable disaster. It was entirely a man-made one. The following quote is taken from an article written in Wikipedia on the causes and impact of the disaster on the local populace:

The cause of the disaster remains until today, under debate. The Indian government and local activists argue that slack management and deferred maintenance created a situation where routine pipe maintenance caused a backflow of water into a MIC tank triggering the disaster. Union Carbide however contends that water entered the tank through an act of sabotage. Even till now very little of the compensation paid has actually reached the victims, decontamination of the ground still not done, causing further suffering, since the terrain is contaminated with mercury and other carcinogenic substances.

Clearly greed and corruption has played a key part in this disaster since how could such a plant, harbouring dangerous chemicals, be allowed to operate close to a large population centre, without stringent safety measures put into place. There are many such disasters waiting to happen, as long as those empowered to safeguard the lives and rights of the people who have placed their trust in them, turn a blind eye and allow themselves to be taken in by their own greed and corrupt practices.

An honest and straight forward leader must be one who not only must be clean but must also be seen to be clean. Personal integrity is demonstrated by who we are and what we do when no one is looking.

I arrived in Johor Bahru in 1989, a young man from the northern state of Perak trying to make a life with my wife and 1 month old son. Qualified as a fledgling civil engineer, I was posted to this southern city in Malaysia as a site engineer for some road construction works.

During this time I saw the many poor practices by the site managers within the company and also by the client representatives themselves. This caused many costly reworks which not only delayed the project but also caused inconvenience to road users. The contract was ultimately terminated and the project awarded to another. Lack of integrity by leadership lead to a disastrous failure of the project and affected the reputation of the company in the long run.

As I progressed later on in my career in other organizations I saw what the effect of lack of integrity caused in the organizations I worked for and the downfall ofmany of my colleagues and top leadership. In the last 30 years, I have seen many management changes averaging around 1 for every 6 years of service, and requiring costly organizational restructuring. The effect of lack of integrity by leaders affects everyone within an organization.

Temptation will always be there for everyone. But a man of integrity will draw the line and always stand up for his principles rooted on integrity and not cross it whatever the cost.

Malaysia is now well known for the many corruption scandals which have been hitting the nation. Transparency International Corruption Perception Index (CPI) ranked Malaysia as 55th among 176 countries in 2015. In 2020 it ranks 57th among 180 countries. In the Malaysian context, opportunity to be involved in corruption mostly occurs in the government sector due to 3 factors which link to corrupt acts namely power, opportunity and moral impurity. On CPI, Malaysia was ranked 3rd in the region below Singapore and Brunei. Quoting from an article written by columnist Azmi Dzof in star2.com,

> Corruption was a large problem in Singapore in the 1970's. It was finally brought under control through the diligent and hard work of the Corrupt Practices Investigation Bureau (CPIB) and the strong political will of the Singapore Government which ascribed a holistic "4A" programme of effective Acts, Agencies, Adjudication and Administration. A strong political will allowed the CPIB to impose its authority. Government processes were simplified, and this resulted in making it difficult to circumvent a now-efficient system which had checks and balances in place whilst at the same time making the general

public see it as a good return for their tax dollars."Corruption is the creation of time and discretion," said the co-chairman of Malaysia's Special Task Force to Facilitate Business - PEMUDAH (taken from the task force's Malay name "Pasukan Pertugas Khas Pemudahcara Perniagaan"), at the time. "You limit the time and take away the discretion, you eradicate corruption." Although PEMUDAH was tasked to improve efficiency, a key to achieving this was to reduce corruption.

Today the government has set up Urban Transformation Centers (UTC) at many shopping malls and other convenient locations throughout cities and rural areas which are like one stop centers for the people to renew, for example, passports and driving licenses and pay utility bills. What used to take a whole day or a few days, now takes only a few hours and can be done in a comfortable environment. This releases huge crowds from the centers of government departments which could cause discomfort and even security concerns, among others.

So a change in environment can affect culture. A country seen overhauling weak institutions and systems will also raise public confidence. Most importantly the key institutions within the country must be allowed to function without interference from the political elite. When politicians try to politicize key civil service institutions and systems for their own self interest, it invariably leads to its dilution and ultimately weakens it leading to disruptions within the nation as a whole and gives rise to discontent within the people due to the rise in corruption and other injustices.

Why are the names of some people enshrined in our memories. People like Martin Luther King, Mahatma Gandhi, Mother Teresa will forever shine in the eyes of the people of the world. Self-seekers in the corridors of power and status, fame and name, may become prominent in the eyes of people for some time, but soon they fade from public memory. Honest and straight forward leaders have a mission and purpose in life which transcends their own self-interest. They move out of their comfort zones and embrace the larger world of people and their concerns and dedicate their work for the greater good. They are God-centric people.

In his final moments, Gandhi was feebly walking from Birla house in Delhi towards the Birla grounds, after breaking his fast, supported by his nieces, Manu and Abha who he affectionately called his walking sticks, to lead evening prayers. He was shot three times by his assassin, Naturam Godse. All three shots hit Gandhi in his chest. As he collapsed, his lips moved and they, as they did a thousand times before uttered, "He Ram!" (O' God!). He had attained unison with his creator having found a meaning to live and a meaning to die. A leader of integrity must have the courage to risk his or her job, and refuse to stand by and allow corrupt practices from eating into the organization, even if everyone else is looking the other way.

A leader who is greedy for bribes tears down the company and causes misery to its people. The same applies to a country and your family.

CHAPTER 15-
OVERSEE EFFECTIVE SUPERVISION

"Taking responsibility is worth the effort, it even saves lives!"

Towards the end of my active career within the oil and gas and marine industry, I was appointed as the senior transformation leader within the organization which was at that time undergoing great upheaval. The organization had appointed a consultant to look into the weaknesses within and to come out with improvements to transform the company to meet the challenges in the global market. It was a do or die situation. The workforce was adequate for the jobs at hand but somehow things were not going in the right direction. The company was losing millions in lost or misplaced materials. There seemed to be a lot of repeat purchases of materials which had been misplaced. Subcontractors were running the work sites and company supervisors could hardly be seen at site after lunch. Errors in purchasing and mistakes in material take-offs by engineers, was costing the company both in monetary terms and in reputation. There was no pride and joy by employees in carrying out their work effectively. The Company brand was failing when at one time it was the preferred brand to customers.

The value of work should be learned at an early age. Do all you can to help boys and girls discover the joy of work. As Thomas Jefferson said, "It is while we are young that the habit of industry is formed, if not then it never is afterwards. The fortune of our lives therefore depends on employing well the short period of youth."

Coming back to the earlier story, the company was failing due to its very success. Employees were of the opinion that since this was a large government linked corporation (GLC), there would again be a bail-out and that customers linked to the government would continue awarding jobs to the company. Everything would be nice and dandy and their jobs secured. Hence the first thing to do was to remove this fallacy and impart on all levels of staff that we should not be afraid of giving too much of ourselves to our job. We should not measure our work by the salary but rather by the measure of love we can give to our job. We must not be satisfied with our present record of achievement but to understand that if we never do more than we can get paid for, we will never get paid for more than we do. In short the message sent across the board was simple, "If we stopped paddling, we will surely sink". The spirit needed to be put back into the job.

Working for gain is creditable to a man, since it enables him to earn an honourable livelihood. Every person who works for a living can add meaning and purpose to his work if he regards it as not only a means of earning, but also as an opportunity to contribute to the wellbeing of others. By his labour, the worker joins his fellow men and serves them and becomes a partner in the work of bringing God's creation to perfection.

The enjoyment of work depends upon the manner in which the individual accepts its challenge. When a man embarks on a task with a light heart and the will to win,
he is almost certain to enjoy his endeavour's. But if he attacks it half-heartedly, fearfully and wrought with self-doubt, his labours become an intolerable burden.

Many within the organization were just satisfied with a steady or high paying job, neglecting to understand that their mediocre work was costing the company in terms of its reputation and its profitability. It was important for everyone to understand that the only important thing was to do one's job well and with minimal mistakes and perform with the highest quality. They needed to learn to accept responsibility, appraise their own performance honestly and attempt to manage themselves before trying to manage others.

By taking responsibility, we may also save someone's life. In the year 1988, as a young project engineer in charge of a work site, my job was to oversee the construction of water treatment plants to improve the quality of water supplied to the local population. Part of this construction work required pipe laying works from the water treatment plant. As we were digging the ground using a mechanical digger and laying the pipes, we approached a certain stretch of ground with loose sandy soil. The only way to continue was to either send in workers to dig the soil manually and shore up the side with wood or to employ very costly steel sheet piling.

Conveying the situation to my head office, I was instructed to continue with the operation using workers digging manually. The company was not willing to spend the additional cost for steel sheet piling since there was no budget. The site was in a dilemma. We knew that sending workers in could endanger their lives and we were not willing to allow that. We collectively took the decision to continue digging using the mechanical digger to the depth possible and continue laying the pipes even though it was not as per the required depth and alignment. I knew that water supplied from the elevated tank would be able to push through under gravity even with the unevenly aligned pipes at that point.

Hence a simple calculated compromise made together with

the client site supervisor resolved a somewhat sticky situation and the work continued without having to send workers into the trench and endangering their lives.

Many years later a similar situation was repeated at our oil and gas fabrication yard but with disastrous consequences. A vessel (tank) was being commissioned on the deck of an offshore topside structure under construction. Since a vessel is considered to be confined space, anyone wishing to enter into the vessel to carry out inspections, would have to comply with the confined space safety procedures. A Canadian supplier representative was standing by with two young technicians to go into the vessel to inspect its interior prior to commissioning activities. The manholes had already been opened to release any toxic fumes or gases which could have been inside. While waiting for the safety officer to conduct the final gas check, he spotted some debris at the bottom of the vessel. He gestured towards the two technicians and one of them started climbing down the ladder, into the tank, to remove the debris.

The supplier representative did not consider it to be his responsibility to intervene and stop the young technician from going in. Disaster struck almost immediately and the technician collapsed inside. The second technician, seeing his colleague in difficulty, immediately jumped in to save him, but he too collapsed. By the time the emergency response team brought them out only one could be revived. The first technician had already lost his life.

As part of the team carrying out the accident investigation it was found that deadly argon welding gas had found its way into the tank. Argon gas being an asphyxiant and being colourless and odourless had sucked out all oxygen from the lungs of the young technician and he fell unconscious before suffocating to death, without him even knowing it. This is how deadly argon gas is. If only the supplier representative had stopped the two young persons from going in and they had waited for the gas check to be conducted first, this tragic accident could have been prevented. A young life had unfortunately been lost, another badly injured and for the Canadian, a lifetime of regret and psychological trauma on knowing that he could have prevented this tragedy by his intervention, but did not.

CAN ANYONE TELL ME....
WHY HQ IS CONCERNED THAT
THERE IS A LACK OF SUPERVISION
HERE AT OUR BRANCH....
BRANCH MANAGER
RONNIE

CHAPTER 16-
NEVER JUMP TO CONCLUSIONS

"What happens next, depends on you!"

Many years ago, my wife and I were attending an orientation programme for engineering students. We were treated to a parenting talk by a guest speaker. It was about building bridges with our children.

Building bridges with the people around us means that we must first overcome our own fears and limitations and try to open up to the people around us. We can start by showing concern. Listening to the person with concern rather than trying to take control of any conversation is the very first step in the task of building this important bridge especially as a parent with your children.

Using words of Concern rather than words which sound like we are taking control of the conversation will set the right path which will then lead to the next important step which is Acceptance. By accepting our own weaknesses and the weaknesses of others, we can then decide the best way to respond to it. If your child has an anger management problem, you need to understand what is causing this state of mind which is leading to bouts of anger whenever you try as a parent to communicate with your child. It could be triggered by the tone of your voice, in the condescending manner in which you speak, or maybe your body language such as watching the television while your child is trying to talk to you. Accepting our own weaknesses rather than avoiding it and pointing fingers at the other person will help lay another important brick in building this bridge.

Respond in the right way rather than reacting in an emotional way. Reacting will not help at all. Rather it will lead to a complete failure in the conversation with the other person. The conversation will either freeze or become confrontational and that would then be the end of it with the person walking away. The conversation now can move into the next final brick which will complete the bridge which we are trying to build. The brick of expanding our communication with the other person.

Expanding is the direct opposite of exclusion. When we expand, we are saying to the other person that we are there for them and will support them in any way we can. By including our children and not pushing them away from us we lay that final important brick to complete the bridge which will last a lifetime and reduce unnecessary pain and heartache which are being faced by so many families today.

The human persona is not easy to understand. When we are talking to a person, we can't really know what's going on inside that person. At some time a person could seem moody and at other times happy. Energy levels fluctuate throughout the day due to stress, lack of rest or sleep or even due to illness. Worry and anxiety, caused by many factors, can cause a person to be not in the right frame of mind. If we can understand that we will then not make that greatest of all mistakes which is to jump to conclusions. Most people will jump to conclusions when they can't understand why the other person is reacting badly against them. The only way to win an argument with anyone is to avoid it in the first place. Hence it's very important to learn to, "Never Jump To Conclusions".

Walk silently, speak softly. Create an environment which is receptive to the other person. Don't argue, demean or shout at the other person. Once you start arguing, you have already lost control of yourself. The whole perspective and the goal of what you set out to do will become lost within the torrents of screaming and fault findings. You will have lost the goal to communicate, to influence, to persuade and motivate the other person. If at all you need to call attention to the other person's faults, do it constructively. Asking questions rather than giving orders will make the other person more receptive to what you are trying to achieve.

The great Russian novelist, Leo Tolstoy, who wrote masterpieces such as *War And Peace*, once said, "Everyone thinks of changing the world, but no one thinks of changing himself." The only person who you can ever change is yourself. This is an absolute fact. However by your own right actions, the people surrounding us will slowly come to the realization of their own actions and will make changes however slowly. Change will then start happening, subtlely at first, and then become visibly noticeable.

CHAPTER 17-
SETTING GOALS

"It's your imagination which turns a molehill into a mountain"

Goals are aims which we set for ourselves which provide the direction in our lives to focus on. Everyone needs to set goals to achieve, if we are not to become aimless in life. Goals must be clear, challenging and achievable. The earlier in life that we set goals, the more successful we will become. The first question we need to ask ourselves is, what is it that we really want to be? Do I want to be an Engineer? If so what sort of engineering field should I take? Is this what interests me? What sort of career will that take me into? Take a reality check and ask whether we are heading in the right direction.

Achievers go after opportunities, they don't wait for them. Everyday chances knock at your door, waiting for your response. Wishful thinkers neither catch them nor create them, they just ignore them. Hence goals are created in our minds which will then lead to focus in achieving the goals set. Make it a habit in taking a pen and notebook and writing down your goals in life. Listing out on a piece of paper the things you want to accomplish in your life. With right planning of goals, life begins at the age of 50 and you will then enjoy the fruits of all your labour and can then do all the things that you dreamt of doing but could not while you were working. Be self reliant and don't begrudge your children for not providing or coming to see you often. They are making a life also. How do you achieve this? By saving enough, carrying out risk management by taking some life and medical insurances for yourself and your family, keeping healthy by exercising and enjoying some leisure activities, going for regular medical screening, interacting with friends and neighbours and finally just be happy with yourself.

Make them important goals such as your career, getting married to the person you love, having good health and achieving financial freedom and buying that dream house in the right location. As times go by the goals could also develop and change since the only certainty in life is change. As life changes, so too your goals. Also keep evaluating your goals as you progress in life. Set short term goals and also long term ones. Always pursue your dreams and continuously make improvements to improve your quality of life. We will make mistakes since we must make decisions. But don't let that discourage you. It is better to make a decision and follow through with it rather than not making any decision at all. We all make decisions everyday of our lives. But setting the right goals and asking the right questions on how we can meet those goals will help us achieve those goals and succeed in life.

Organizations need goals, as much as individuals. Leaders within organizations need to make it a priority for all its heads of departments to set goals which are clear, challenging and achievable. Due to the ever changing business environment, such goals need to be reviewed on a yearly basis. Setting goals and striving to achieve them and tying up such goals to your employees key performance indicators (KPI) will align everyone within the organization to strive for achieving the vision and mission of the organization as a whole. Most organizations will do the planning of goal setting in conjunction with the start of every new financial year. All budgetary estimates required in achieving the departmental targets will need to be planned and factored into the overall Company Management Plans for the year ahead.

Delays in receiving payments for invoices billed to customers, is a common complaint of many suppliers. Such delays, regularly exceeding the mutually agreed payment period, can strain the relationship between suppliers and their customers. Suppliers normally provide their invoices together with their goods delivery order documents which have been verified by the customer's warehouse which is responsible for receiving the goods.

As a Senior Supply Chain Manager, managing the warehouse has always been a challenge. Warehouse personnel would, most of the time, have to bear the brunt of the blame from end users and suppliers for late deliveries of materials due to delays in releasing payments to suppliers, even if the root cause of the problem lied elsewhere. The Finance department responsible for making the timely payments to suppliers would blame the delays in payment release to the delay in invoice verification and approval by the end users. Hence the warehouse would be squeezed between the project teams and finance personnel whenever suppliers delayed supplying the essential goods required for the smooth running of projects due to delays in their invoice payments. Hence we needed to seek a way and devise a method to improve our internal system and stop the blame game which was affecting morale and affecting the smooth running and progress of projects.

Having looked at the way the invoices were being manually circulated without any ownership, we devised a simple method whereby all invoices and documents could be tracked. Firstly suppliers submitting their invoices were required to submit all necessary documents together with their invoices, failing which the finance team was not allowed to receive them in the first place. They were to ensure the completeness of all invoices before receiving them. The clock was to start ticking only from this time onwards. Next step was to have a system to track all invoices circulated and track the time taken by each department, including the warehouse till it reached back to the finance department which originated the distribution process. Finally the time taken to release payments by finance personnel, after receiving verified and approved invoices was also made part of the tracking process. Hence a simple method devised and tied up to the KPI's of respective departments helped to improve the overall process tremendously. Everyone was now happy and projects were able to run smoothly without running out of essential material. Always try to seek a way and devise methods to improve upon what you're doing. Never stop dreaming and never stop trying to seek something different. Even if a project seems too imposing, even impossible, throw your hat over the fence. You will then have to find a way to climb over it to get it. There is nothing which cannot be achieved by the human mind if it sets out to do it. When you make a bold move and put yourself in an untenable situation, you're forced to climb the fence. The next important ingredient in achieving your goals is determination.

Determination is made up of hard work and perseverance. These are the steps to great achievements. Plato said, "I never did anything worth doing by accident, nor did any of my inventions come by accident, they came by work." Behind the attainment of any worthwhile goal is the spirit of determination and a saga of many painful efforts and failures. Life is made up of time. So stop wasting time. Wise living consists of wise use of time. Successful people make the most of every moment, never throwing it away recklessly. They are not necessarily great persons, but they achieve success by perseverance and grit. They have definite goals and the discipline to achieve them. The only person who can stop you from achieving your goals is yourself. You, and only you are your greatest enemy. Hence try to achieve your own potential. Learn to know yourself and not try to be better than the other person. Competing with others is an insane approach. It will only burn you out in the end.

William Faulkner was asked for a formula on being a good novelist. His reply was, "Always dream and shoot higher than you know you can do. Don't bother just to be better than your contemporaries. Try to be better than yourself."

NOW THEN GENTLEMEN ....
LET's SET OUR GOALS...
SHALL WE....
GOALS
1.
2.
3.
4.
5.
ABC PTE LTD

GLOSSARY OF TERMS

Adamant - unyielding; firm in purpose

Adjudicate - give a judgment; or decision upon

Administration - management of affairs, etc, especially public affairs

Adulthood - persons grown to be intellectually and emotionally mature

Adversity - condition of adverse fortune; trouble

Agency - business; place of business, of an agent

Akin - of similar character

Alarming - warning of danger

Align - arrange in a line; into agreement, close co-operation

All ahead full - go forward at full speed

Allegation - statement, especially one made without proof

Amphibious - adapted for both land and sea

Analyze - examine in order to learn what it is made up of

Apportion - divide; distribute; give as a share

Appraisal - valuation

Apt - quick-witted

Architect - a person who designs (and supervises the construction of buildings, etc

Argument - disagreement; quarre

Array - display; order

Arrogance - behaving in a proud, superior manner

Artificial Intelligence - intelligence which is not natural; made by man

Asphyxia - condition caused by lack of enough air in the lungs; suffocation

Assemblage - bringing or coming together; assembly

Augmented - make or become

Autopsy - post - mortem examination of a body (by cutting it open) to learn the cause of death.

Begrudge - feel or show dissatisfaction or envy

Behemoth - something enormous

Berate - scold sharply

Big picture - the most important facts about the situation and the effects of that situation on other things

Biotechnology - the exploitation of biological processes for industrial and other purposes

Blame game - blaming others for something bad or unfortunate rather than attempting to seek a solution

Body language - is a type of non-verbal communication in which physical behaviour such as facial expressions, gestures, eye movement, body posture etc, are used to express or convey information

Brutal - animal-like; cruel and unthinking

Budgetary - estimate of probable future income and expenditure

Campaign - group of military operations with a set purpose

Canyon - deep gorge

Capacity - ability to hold, contain, get hold of, learn things

Casualty - accident, especially one involving loss of life

Catalogue - list of names, places/goods etc, in a special orde

Cavity - empty space; small hole, within a solid body

CEO - Chief Executive Officer

Chaos - complete absence of order

Chide - scold; rebuke

Clarity - clearness

Coined - invent (a new word or phrase)

Colleague - a person with whom one works in a profession or business

Collision - an instance of one moving object or person striking violently against another

Comfort zone - a situation where one feels safe or at ease

Commander - a person in command

Commencement address - speech given to graduating students

Commerce - trade (especially between countries)

Commissioning - order or authorize the production of (something)

Communicate - pass on (news, information, feelings)

Component - *adj* helping to form (a complete thing): *parts*

Concept - idea underlying a class of things; general notion

Condescending - behave graciously, but in a way that shows one's feeling of superiority

Congregation - a group of people assembled for religious worship

Conjure - to do clever tricks which appear magical

Consideration - thinking about

Console - give comfort or sympathy to

Consultant - a person who gives expert advice

Contemporary - belonging to the same time

Cubicle - small division of a larger room, walled or curtained to make a separate compartment

Cues - hint about what to do or say

Degenerate - pass from a state of goodness to a lower state by losing qualities which are considered normal and desirable

Demean - lower oneself in dignity

Depletion - use up

Dick Tracy - American comic strip detective created in 1931

Dictate - state with the force of authority

Digital Age - information age

Dilemma - situation in which one has to choose between two things

Dilution - make weaker or thinner

Discord - disagreement

Dissipate - disappear or cause to disappear

Distribution process - a chain of businesses or intermediaries through which goods or services pass until it reaches the end consumer

Dumping ground - a place where garbage or unwanted material is left

Emanating - originating from

Embroil - to be mixed up in a quarrel

Emergency response - response to mitigate the impact of an incident on the public or environment by trained personnel

Empathetic - understanding and sharing another person's feelings

Engineering - the branch of science and technology concerned with the design, building, and use of engines, machines, and structures; the work done by, or the occupation of, an engineer

Enshrine - preserve (a right, tradition, or idea) in a form that ensures it will be protected and respected

Etch - engrave

Ethnicity - the fact or state of belonging to a social group that has a common national or cultural tradition

Even keel - balanced, as a ship is floating on its designated waterline and the keel is horizontal

Excerpts - take a short extract from a text

Executive - a person with a senior managerial responsibility in a business organization

Fabrication yard - a demarcated area where metal construction which includes but not limited to cutting, grinding, and welding and boring holes to different shapes and configuration

Facilitate - make (an action or process) easy or easier

Facilities department - responsible for the maintenance of an organiza- tion's buildings and equipment

Fallacy - a mistaken belief, especially one based on unsound argument

Flawed - blemished, damaged, or imperfect in some way

Frontier - the extreme limit of human settlement beyond which lies wilderness;

Galvanize - shock or excite (someone), typically into taking action

God-centric - centering on or directed toward God

Handicap - a circumstance that makes progress or success difficult

Hardwired - involving or achieved by permanently connected circuits

Heave - lift or haul (a heavy thing) with great effort

Helter-Skelter - in disorderly haste or confusion

Homily - a religious discourse; a sermon

House of Commons - lower house of Parliament of the United Kingdom

Iceberg - a very large mass of ice that floats in the sea

Image3-D - in a 3-D film or picture, the objects look real and solid instead of looking like a normal flat picture

Industrial - in or related to industry, or having a lot of industry and factories, etc.

Industrial Revolution - the period of time during which work began to be done more by machines in factories than by hand at home

Inferior - lower, or of lower rank someone who is considered to be less important than other people

Initiative - the ability to use your judgment to make decisions and do things without needing to be told what to do

Innovation - (the use of) a new idea or method

Install - to put furniture, a machine, or a piece of equipment into position and make it ready to use

Institute, educational an organization where people do a particular type of educational work, or the buildings that it uses

Instruments - a tool or other device, especially one without electrical power, used for performing a particular piece of work

Integrity - the quality of being honest and having strong moral principles that you refuse to change

Interface - a connection between two pieces of electronic equipment, or between a person and a computer

Interpersonal - connected with relationships between people

Intimidate - to frighten or threaten someone, usually in order to persuade them to do something that you want them to do

Intolerable - too bad or unpleasant to deal with or accept

Invasive - moving into all areas of something and difficult to stop

Invention - something that has never been made before, or the process of creating something that has never been made before

Invoice - a list of things provided or work done together with their cost, for payment at a later time

Jacket Structure - substructure or foundation of an offshore oil and gas platform which is fixed to the seabed

Jetty - a wooden or stone structure built in the water at the edge of a sea or lake and used by people getting on and off boats

Juggernaut - a large powerful force or organization that cannot be stopped

Juggle - to succeed in arranging your life so that you have time to involve yourself in two or more different activities or groups of people:

Key Performance Indicator (KPI) - a way of measuring a company's progress towards the goals it is trying to achieve

Lamentable - deserving severe criticism; very bad

Lepers - a person suffering from leprosy

Levitate - to (cause to) rise and float in the air without any physical support

Lifeform - any living thing

Limitations - the act of controlling and especially reducing something

Line Manager - the person who is directly responsible for managing the work of someone else in a company or business, and who is one level above that person

Load-out - the transfer of an object onto a vessel or vehicle

Mandatory - Something that is mandatory must be done, or is demanded by law

Marine industry - industry which undertakes the building of boats, ships, oil rigs etc

Market, global - all the people in all areas of the world who buy or might want to buy something

Marvels - a thing or person that is very surprising or causes a lot of admiration

Mass - a large amount of something that has no particular shape or arrangement

Mediocre - not very good

Meditation - the act of giving your attention to only one thing, either as a religious activity or as a way of becoming calm and relaxed

Mentor - a person who gives a younger or less experienced person help and advice over a period of time, especially at work or school

Microchip - a very small piece of semiconductor, especially in a computer, that contains extremely small electronic circuits and devices, and can perform particular operations

Miniature - used to describe something that is a very small copy of an object

Minions - a person who has to do what another person of higher rank orders them to do

Momentum - the force that keeps an object moving or keeps an event developing after it has started

Monstrous - something that is very ugly and usually large

Mooring system - the ropes or chains that keep a boat from moving away from a particular place

Moralize - to express judgments about what is morally right and wrong

Motto - a short sentence or phrase that expresses a belief or purpose

Mystic - a person who seeks union with God and, through that, realization of truth beyond men's understanding

Native - relating to the first people to live in an area

Network - a large system consisting of many similar parts that are connected together to allow movement or communication between or along the parts, or between the parts and a control centre

Neurosurgeon - a doctor who performs operations involving the brain or nerves

Nip - pinch, squeeze, or bite sharply

Noble - moral in an honest, brave, and kind way

Novelist - a person who writes novels

Nurture - to help a plan or a person to develop and be successful

Oceangoing - of a ship, boat, etc, designed for travelling across large areas of ocean

Offshore oil & gas platform - a large structure that carries equipment that is used to get oil and gas from under the sea

Oil Industry - the companies and activities involved in the process of producing oil

Oncology - the study and treatment of tumours (= masses of cells) in the body

Onshore - moving towards land from the sea, or on land rather than at sea

Operating Table - a special table that a patient lies on during an operation

Order book - a book in which a business keeps a record of customers' orders

Orientation programme - training or preparation for a new job or activity

Overhaul - to repair or improve something so that every part of it works as it should

Partition - a vertical structure like a thin wall that separates one part of a room or building from another

Personnel - the people who are employed in a company, organization, or one of the armed forces

Persuasive - making you want to do or believe a particular thing

Phenomenal - extremely successful or special, especially in a surprising way

Philosopher - someone who studies or writes about the meaning of life

Phrase - a group of words that is part of, rather than the whole of, a

sentence

Poet - a person who writes poems

Politicize - to make something or someone political, or more involved in or conscious of political matters

Populace - the ordinary people who live in a particular country or place

Port - left-hand side of a vessel or aircraft, facing forward

Post-mortem - a discussion of an event after it has happened, especially of what was wrong with it or why it failed

Precarious - in a dangerous state because of not being safe or not being held in place firmly

Prerequisite - something that must exist or happen before something else can exist or happen

Prevail - to get control or influence

Principle- a general truth used as a basis of reasoning

or action

Procurement - the process of getting supplies

Productivity - the rate at which a company or country makes goods, usually judged in connection with the number of people and the amount of materials necessary to produce the goods

Profit margin - the difference between the total cost of making and selling something and the price it is sold for

Prominent - very well known and important

Psychologist - someone who studies the human mind and human emotions and behaviour, and how different situations have an effect on people

Psychology - the scientific study of the way the human mind works and how it influences behaviour, or the influence of a particular person's character on their behaviour

Pull rank - to use the power that your position gives you over someone in order to make them do what you want

Pulpit - a raised place in a church, with steps leading up to it, from which the priest or minister speaks to the people during a religious ceremony

Quotient - a particular degree or amount of something

Realization - the fact or moment of starting to understand a situation

Recondition - to repair a machine or piece of equipment and return it to a good condition

Rectify - to correct something or make something right

Regimen - any set of rules about food and exercise that someone follows, especially in order to improve their health

Rehabilitation - the process of returning to a healthy or good way of life, or the process of helping someone to do this after they have been in prison, been very ill, etc

Relish - to like or enjoy something

Remarshall - bring together

Resentment - to feel angry because you have been forced to accept someone or something that you do not like

Resolve - to solve or end a problem or difficulty

Restraint - calm and controlled behaviour

Retrenchment - a situation in which someone loses their job because their employer does not need them

Revolution - a change in the way a country is governed, usually to a different political system and often using violence or war

Rife - If something unpleasant is rife, it is very common or happens a lot

Sabotage - to intentionally prevent the success of a plan or action

Sage - wise, especially as a result of great experience

Saint - a person who has received an official honour from the Christian, especially the Roman Catholic, Church for having lived in a good and holy way

Sanctuary - protection or a safe place, especially for someone or something being chased or hunted

Scapegoat - a person who is blamed for something that someone else has done

Scarce - not easy to find or get

Screening - a test or examination to discover if there is anything wrong with someone

Sedentary - involving little exercise or physical activity

Self discipline - the ability to make yourself do things you know you should do even when you do not want to

Self reliant - not needing help or support from other people

Self-esteem - belief and confidence in your own ability and value

Self-Fulfilling prophesy - something that you cause to happen by saying and expecting that it will happen

Self-seeking - interested in your own advantage in everything that you do

Serenity - peaceful and calm; worried by nothing

Service industry - an industry that provides a service for people but does not result in the production of goods

Shareholders - a person who owns shares in a company and therefore gets part of the company's profits and the right to vote on how the company is controlled

Site - a place where something is, was, or will be built, or where something happened, is happening, or will happen

Social - relating to activities in which you meet and spend time with other people and that happen during the time when you are not working

Software - the instructions that control what a computer does; computer programs

Solace - help and comfort when you are feeling sad or worried

Solar System - the sun and the group of planets that move around it

Sophisticated - intelligent or made in a complicated way and therefore able to do complicated tasks

Spiritual - relating to deep feelings and beliefs, especially religious beliefs

Starboard - the right side of a ship or aircraft as you are facing forward

Status - the amount of respect, admiration, or importance given to a person, organization, or object

Sterilize - to make something completely clean and free from bacteria

Stress - great worry caused by a difficult situation, or something that causes this condition

Substructure - a firm structure that supports something built on top of it

Suffocate - to (cause someone to) die because of not having enough oxygen

Supply Chain Process - the system of people and things that are involved in getting a product from the place where it is made to the person who buys it

Sway - to move slowly from side to side

System, circulatory - relating to the system that moves blood through the body and that includes the heart, arteries, and veins

Task force - a group of people who are brought together to do a particular job, or a large military group who have a military aim to achieve

Tax dollar - money collected in taxes, often used to talk about government spending

Tenacity - the determination to continue what you are doing

Theologian - a student of theology

Tilting - to (cause to) move into a sloping position

Timeliness - happening at the best possible moment

Tone - a vocal sound with reference to its pitch, quality, and strength

Tony Stark - Marvel's comic strip (movie) superhero named Iron Man

Top Management - the most important executives in an organization, considered as a group

Topple - to (cause to) lose balance and fall down

Topside - Superstructure of an oil and gas platform

Toxic fumes - poisonous gases

Trainees - a person who is learning and practicing the skills of a particular job

Transcend - to go further, rise above, or be more important or better than something

Transform - to change completely the appearance or character of something or someone, especially so that that thing or person is improved

Transparency - the quality of being done in an open way without secrets

Transverse beam - a beam situated or lying across

Trauma - severe emotional shock and pain caused by an extremely upsetting experience

Tremor - a slight earthquake

Trivial - having little value or importance

Tug (boat) - small powerful boat for towing ships , etc

Tumour - a mass of diseased cells that might become a lump or cause illness

Tyranny - a situation in which someone or something controls how you are able to live, in an unfair way

Ultimatum - a threat in which a person or group of people are warned that if they do not do a particular thing, something unpleasant will happen to them. It is usually the last and most extreme in a series of actions taken to bring about a particular result

Unchartered - An uncharted place or situation is completely new and therefore has never been described before:

Underestimate - to fail to guess or understand the real cost, size, difficulty, etc. of something

Unfold - If a situation or story unfolds, it develops or becomes clear to other people

Unison - acting or speaking together, or at the same time

Unstinting - extremely generous with time, money, praise, help, etc

Untapped - not yet used or taken advantage of

Upheaval - a great change, especially causing or involving much difficulty, activity, or trouble

USD - United States Dollar; currency of the United States of America

Utility - a service that is used by the public, such as an electricity or gas supply or a train service

Vagaries - unexpected events or changes that cannot be controlled and can influence a situation

Values - the principles that help you to decide what is right and wrong, and how to act in various situations

Vast - extremely big

Verbal - of or in words

Verify - to prove that something exists or is true, or to make certain that something is correct

Vision - the ability to imagine how a country, society, industry, etc. could develop in the future and to plan for this

Walkie-talkie - a small radio held in the hand, used for both sending and receiving messages

Warehouse - a large building for storing things before they are sold, used, or sent out to shops

Welding - the activity of joining metal parts together

Wellbeing - the state of feeling healthy and happy

Well-rounded - involving or having experience in a wide range of ideas or activities

Wheat - a plant whose yellowish-brown grain is used for making flour, or the grain itself

Workaholic - a person who works a lot of the time and finds it difficult not to work

Workforce - the group of people who work in a company, industry, country, etc.

Zeal - great enthusiasm or eagerness

BIBLIOGRAPHY

Azmi, Dzof. Is corruption nurture or nature. star2.com, 2015.

Beck, Dr. Aaron T. Cognitive Behavior Therapy (CBT). University of Pennsylvania, 1960 www.beckinstitute.org/cognitive model

Carnegie, Dale. The Leader In You. New York : Pocket Books, 1995. Charmaine, Ng.

Cancer : How to cope : 2016.

Chin, Tarcisius Professor Dr. Living longer, healthier and happier : Ruminating with De La Salle (Year Unknown).

Collins, Jim. How The Mighty Fall. New York : Harper Collins, 2009. Davis, Jack & Bartolo,

Dick De. The Return of a Mad look at old Movies.

New York : E.C. Publications, 1970.

Godfrey, Jason. AI is coming, AI is coming. star2.com, 2016.

Guareschi, Giovanni. Don Camillo's Dilemma. Hammondswath, Middlesex, England : Penguin Books, 1962.

Hart, B.H. Liddell. History of the Second World War. London : Pan Books, 2011.

Malaysian Mouth and Foot Painting Artists Association. Newsletter, 2016.

Margerison, Charles & McCann, Dick. Team Management Systems. Milton, Australia : 2007-2011.

Maurus, J.The Joy of Being Human. Bombay : The Bombay St. Paul Society, 2007. Merton, Robert K.

The Self-Fulfilling Prophecy. Antioch Review, 1948

www.thoughtco.co

Myers, Peter B. & Myers, Katharine D. Myers-Briggs Type Indicator Step II. USA : CPP, 2001, 2003.

Naylon. Cartoonstock.com & pinterest.

Wahl-Immel, Yuriko. No more shaky scapels. star2.com, 2017.

Waterman, Judith A. & Rogers, Jenny. Introduction to the Firo-B Instrument. Mountain View, CA : CPP, 1996, 2004.

AFTERWORD

All leadership is flawed in one way or the other. There is no perfect leader but good leaders always strive to understand how they can grow and foster growth around them. The work of leadership starts with the hard and painful work we must do on ourselves. To build on the things we most value rather than allowing our past insecurities, caused by a mental image of someone from earlier in our lives that influences our behaviour today, to stop our own growth.

Hence the story of the elderly Native American grandfather narrating the tale of the two wolfs to his grandchildren, in the introductory chapter of this book, could also be a story of flawed leadership. Our trials do not come at random. God allows us to go through hard times so that we may grow to become better. His goal is for us to become a reflection of him that not only he can see, but also so others can see him in us.

A secret about good leaders is that they always strive to be who they should be-people who model shared values, inspire with vision and elevate others-and this is what makes them admired by followers and enemies alike. They focus on feeding the good and noble wolf inside of them.

Hope you enjoyed reading this book as much as I enjoyed writing it for you!

◆ ◆ ◆

ACKNOWLEDGEMENT

Thanks to the writers and thinkers, who shaped my thoughts to write this book.

Thanks to my fellow past colleagues for the many contributions given knowingly and unknowingly. The project began in 2014 and was born out of a need to put my thoughts on paper to help aspiring young leaders of today to understand themselves better and to be able to cope with today's ever changing and demanding world.

Thanks to Bernard Wong who pointed me in the right direction. You helped to lay the markers which I could follow along this path to achieving this project.

Thanks to my two children Andrew Roshan and Angela Rachel for reading my manuscript and giving me
their critical acclaim. Angela assisted in the preparation of the glossary of terms and incorporated certain psychological references in addition to editing part of the manuscript. Andrew provided valuable advice on the citations and Bibliography preparation. They are both young aspiring leaders breaking new ground in their own careers in the exciting field of psychology and I am immensely grateful for their support and encouragement.

Finally thanks to my caring, loving, and supportive wife Kiran

Francis, who journeyed together with me along this untrodden path on my quest to find the right support and people in getting this project together and helping me by asking the right questions and for the patience in letting me spend the time to write this book, while you quietly took care of the home. Thanks for the encouragement when the times got tough. My deepest gratitude to you.

ABOUT THE AUTHOR

Ronnie Francis

The writer is a former Engineer with about 30 years of experience in various fields within the Civil Engineering and Oil and Gas Fabrication Industry. He has a wide range of Construction and Management experience and has been a leader within some of Malaysia's largest multinational corporations. He did his schooling at St. Michael's Institution in Ipoh, Malaysia and went on to graduate with a degree in Civil Engineering from The  National Institute of Technology,Bhopal, India. He has a Post Graduate Diploma in Strategic Management from University Technology Malaysia's International Business School. He is also a talented artist and has done many works depicting the rich local cultural and historical heritage and enjoys sketching humorous caricatures depicting people in daily life situations, some of which have been added at the end of each chapter of this book.

This book has been written to help leaders especially the young and aspiring ones to better understand themselves first by learning to accept and understand what makes them tick. Only then can one understand those around us. In a fractionalized and divided world, good leadership qualities are needed, like never before, to create a new and better world. As the writer aptly puts, the key to sucess and happiness lies within us and we must look for it with humility. This book is about our human mind which is truly the

Final Frontier.

His second book 'Growing together in Marriage' has been published in 2021 and has been made available on Amazon Kindle as a digital and paperback edition. This second book has been written to give insight and understanding into the challenges facing married couples, ways to overcome them and keep love alive till the end.
The Author is also an avid environmentalist and a technocrat who regularly posts and shares articles on his LinkedIn profile on issues such as climate change, leadership, mental health and interesting technology. He believes that with right leadership skills and the responsible use of technology we can make this world a better and more inclusive one for all living things.

BOOKS BY THIS AUTHOR

Growing Together In Marriage

Growing Together in Marriage, the authors second book, is about the important principles and concepts needed for a marriage to succeed. Much of the content comes from his three decades of marriage and family life. The book provides insights into understanding the challenges facing married couples, ways to overcome them and what is needed to keep the fire of love alive till the very end. The book is filled with down-to-earth accounts from couples who have shared their marriage experiences. The author has made references to studies conducted by a few well-known psychologists, marriage councellors and discusses the link between temperament and personal character, to deal with our different natures. As the Author aptly points out, Marriage is truly a Miracle created by God, and placed in our own hands to nurture and keep alive. God created Marriage for his Glory and our joy and happiness here and in eternity. Married couples need to understand this so as not to allow it to deteriorate into something unacceptable which can kill the relationship.

This book identifies the specific principles, concepts and emotions in marriage such as, love and dignity, knowing ourselves and learning to know our partner, expectations in marriage, respecting and appreciating your partner, dangers of negative criticism and making assumptions, having a positive sense of humour, willingness to communicate, economic anxiety, romance and sexuality. Each of these topics are treated in a separate chapter and written in simple language. Cartoons shed a humorous light on these aspects.

In marriage we have the greatest of all leadership challenge and couples need to rise to this challenge in their daily lives working together as one. By reading this book, the reader will be able to gain a fuller understanding of oneself and what it takes to understand your spouse for a harmonious and happy marriage life which will withstand the many life changing moments which will come with it making your relationship grow from strength to strength and give inspiration to your own children and others.

Growing Together in Marriage is a book about finding lifetime happiness in your marriage.